D1485607

SOCIAL POLICY AND CITIZENSHIP

SOCIAL POLICY
AND CITIZENSHIP

Julia Parker

Lecturer in the Department of Social and
Administrative Studies, University of Oxford

First published 1975 by
THE MACMILLAN PRESS LTD
London and Basingstoke
Associated companies in New York Dublin
Melbourne Johannesburg and Madras

SBN 333 18093 3 (hard cover)
      333 18094 1 (paper cover)

Printed in Great Britain by
THE ANCHOR PRESS LTD
Tiptree, Essex

Contents

Tables

Introduction

There are many ways of writing about social policy and administration but two kinds of approach have been and are particularly favoured. On the one hand the subject may be treated historically, a perspective which has many dangers. All too often it has meant a recital of successive pieces of social legislation directed to particular problems with the implicit assumption of steady progress towards a more humane society from which poverty has been abolished. Thus we learn about feudalism, where a rigid social hierarchy provided some measure of security for the poor in return for their services, of the Elizabethan statutes which tried to tackle problems of economic and demographic change by setting the unemployed to work, punishing vagrants and supporting the sick and helpless, of the New Poor Law of 1834 which attempted to destroy pauperism by the repressive policies of less eligibility and deterrence, and finally of the welfare state, denoting a humane, enlightened and egalitarian society where poverty has virtually ceased to exist. This happy evolutionary process has, of course, been challenged by sceptics, particularly over the last twenty years, who refuse to admit the disappearance of the most acute material poverty as a measure of social progress, who emphasise the scandal of any degree of poverty in a rich society and who point to the gross inequalities in living standards and opportunities that persist in advanced industrial countries. There is, of course, a very different kind of historical enquiry, which attempts to identify the circumstances, interests and values influencing the development of welfare legislation, and which is vitally important in any comprehensive study of social policy.

The second kind of approach eschews the historical perspective and concentrates on the objectives, structure, responsibilities and administrative procedures of the various organisations, both statutory and voluntary, which are concerned with welfare. At its best this kind of study supplies the essential factual basis for analysing the aims and principles of social provision, for evaluating its consequences and detecting its problems. It is the stuff of which theories, if not dreams, are made. At its worst, however, it becomes a minutely detailed description, without any historical, analytical or theoretical reference, of the legislation which makes up the welfare state and of the way in which that legislation is implemented. This kind of information is necessary for social workers and administrators, but it is not in itself a proper object of attention in the academic study of social policy. It calls to mind the stern warning which decorates the walls of Manchester's Central Reference Library: 'Where is the wisdom that is lost in understanding, where is the understanding that is lost in knowledge, where is the knowledge that is lost in information?'

The purpose of this book is neither to trace the development of welfare legislation nor to describe in comprehensive detail the present arrangements. The study of social policy is here conceived as an examination of the way in which a range of goods and services – income, health, education – which are highly significant for personal well-being, are socially distributed, and in particular of the part government policies play in that distribution. The book has three aims: to set out a theoretical approach to the academic study of social policy, to examine British arrangements in terms of that approach, and to point to the problems involved in developing a system which attempts to relate services to need.

In the first instance, and as a step towards a theoretical frame of reference, I outline three possible welfare models, each embodying a distinctive approach to questions of social distribution based on different principles which have varying implications for government policy. Special attention is paid to the third or socialist model in which need, linked to the idea of citizenship, is the most important criterion for distribution.

The concepts of need, demand and supply are used throughout the book with reference to welfare and the social services. All three words have the vagueness and convenience of common speech: all three require an anticipatory remark of clarification and warning here. Supply and demand, as economists use these terms, have a familiar and precise meaning in the context of market exchange. In a perfect market supply is determined by owners' or manufacturers' decisions according to their judgements of relative value, and demand is similarly determined by the judgements of consumers, the two being adjusted to one another by price. The conditions of a free market do not, however, obtain with regard to welfare goods and services. On the supply side there is the state, which may monopolise or dominate provision and which operates through a bureaucracy backed by law or established administrative practice. The state, moreover, is not bound by direct considerations of marginal profitability. It may be required by law to provide a service or impose a standard, though it may at the same time have regard to economic costs, cost effectiveness or cost–benefit calculations, and it may be in competition with private market supplies as, for example, in health or education. Moreover, still on the supply side, welfare is also a function of kinship, neighbourly and community activity generated by neither law nor profit but by custom, usage, kindliness or social obligation – all forces whose sway over human behaviour may change with changing social conditions. In other words, both markets and bureaucracies operate in the context of particular social structures. The quantity and quality of the welfare they supply will consequently vary.

In a similar way, social and economic conditions constrain the quality and quantity of what is demanded. Familes may be more or less scattered and more or less reliable in supporting their members. Legal entitlement may be more or less known, more or less stigmatised, and appeals for assistance more or less encouraged by state or private agencies. Income distribution may be more or less unequal and so give rise to fluctuating statutory entitlement, for example to supplementary benefits or to unemployment pay.

The concept of need has to be analysed before relating it to either demand or supply. It may be given a physiological meaning as 'X' calories per day for the maintenance of physical efficiency. Or it may have a quasi-objective social meaning in relation to the established norms of, say, housing, clothing or diet of a given country. It may also have a subjective meaning as a rich man may be poor or at least 'relatively deprived' in his own estimation and with regard to particular reference groups. Thus a wide range of meanings exists. For the purposes of this book the term is used in a restricted sense to denote two relevant considerations. First, it refers to a criterion which may be used in a non-market situation for political decisions about supply and for the legal or administrative recognition of demand. Thus, in health, the doctor is licensed to assess medical need and to distribute his 'doctor's orders' accordingly. His authority is constrained, in the case of the National Health Service, by established powers and preferences which determine what resources shall be available for particular medical purposes (for example surgery as against geriatric care) and ultimately by the total resources allocated to the Health Service from the public purse. But distribution in that context of the objective variations in people's circumstances with respect

Second, the word 'need' has a meaning distinct from 'demand' in the context of the objective variations in people's circumstances with respect to standards of health, housing, social security, child care and individual well-being. Industrialisation, modernisation, urbanisation, egalitarian values – all represent changing conditions of human need in the sense in which the term is used below. Where neither family nor community nor market meet the social demands which are generated and recognised by a society, varying pressures develop for different kinds of public intervention. Professions arise, among them the social-work profession, with claims, more or less valid, exact and accepted, to assess and deal with the needs of people. Underlying the law and practice of their activities are principles of social policy which relate need on the one hand to supply and demand on the other.

In many ways welfare needs are engendered or intensified by the character of industrial organisation. Industrial development often entails long hours of work, insanitary working conditions, squalid domestic housing and poor amenities, all of which pose a threat to health which is met sooner or later by government action to compel minimum standards. Fluctuations in trade as well as changing methods of production lead to unemployment and redundancy, a threat to the incomes of workers which may be countered by some kind of income-maintenance programme or, generally at a later stage of development, by government intervention in the economy to maintain a given level of employment. At the same time, advances in scientific and technological knowledge lead to new industrial techniques and demands for educated and skilled workers. Thus the appropriate training for employment becomes an important need in industrial countries.

Developments in science and technology both change industrial processes and also affect other areas of knowledge. The combination of increased economic resources and increased scientific understanding opens up increased possibilities of tackling an ever wider range of social problems. Hence new needs for social intervention are created, for example in medicine, as it becomes possible to treat conditions earlier regarded as unchangeable. The peculiar needs created by industrialisation are, then, partly the result of hardships imposed by the economic system and partly the result, paradoxically, of the greater resources that can be devoted to investigating and remedying an increasing variety of social problems.

The need for public social-security and welfare arrangements is affected by family and social structure as well as by the form of industrial organisation. The type of family most commonly found in rich industrial countries is the nuclear group of parents and dependent children, a unit not always completely equipped to provide material security and support for its members in face of the hazards associated with an industrial economy. Finally, various aspects of social structure — economic, political, social, racial and ethnic differences — may all have important implications for need or demand for public-security and welfare programmes.

In the second part of the book the three welfare models are used to analyse the British system, and especially to determine how far British arrangements are consistent with the values inherent in the socialist model. The analysis shows that in practice the distribution of goods and services in Britain is associated very tenuously with need; other factors such as class, family background, geography and professional interests are often more important in determining standards of living and opportunities.

There are various explanations for the failure to realise a distribution based on the idea of citizenship. Fundamental, perhaps, is a lack of political will or power. Both power and will can, however, be changed and the question therefore arises as to what kind of public policies would in fact be required to bring about a system where supply was closely related to need. This is the subject of the third part of the book, which discusses such crucial matters as the significance of selective and universal services, the question of democratic control and participation in policy-making and the importance of planning and research in relation to setting objectives, establishing priorities, measuring needs and assessing the quality of public provision.

PART I

Social Policy and Social Structure

CHAPTER 1

Models of Welfare

In the rich industrial countries poverty is now more usually defined in
sociological rather than in physiological terms; in relation to the variation in living standards within a particular society rather than in
relation to a concept of what is necessary to maintain physical health.
Persons or families are classified as poor according to the degree to
which their standard of living falls below the average. This does not
mean that poverty in the absolute sense has disappeared; only that it is
less common than in 1899 when Rowntree found nearly 30 per cent of
the population of York living below the physical efficiency level.
Perhaps it would be better to speak of a new problem – inequality –
emerging as a matter of public concern and of public policy, rather than
that of poverty being redefined. But however it is expressed the sub-
stance of the change is clear : great inequalities in living conditions and
in opportunities, as well as absolute destitution, are held to justify
government intervention. There is plenty of room, of course, for disagreement about the amount and kind of inequality that is acceptable;
there will be many different views about the proper definition and
measure of poverty even though the subsistence idea is widely rejected.[1]

Thus, there is no automatic response to a given set of demonstrated
needs. Lack of resources drastically limits the chances of poor countries
to develop welfare systems, but there are wide differences in the policies
of the rich countries with a similar level of wealth and confronted by
similar problems. This is hardly surprising. Needs have to be recognised
before programmes are devised to meet them; this is partly a matter of
empirical knowledge but also a question of power relations, of values,
and the availability of the means to supply them. The situation of
individuals or groups is defined as representing need and calling for
government action in the light of different theories about the causes,
nature and consequences of poverty, and different convictions about the
kind of political, economic and social relations between men and women
that are desirable. Not that public policies are ever entirely determined
by ideas. They are vitally affected by the interests of the economically

and politically powerful. It is a matter for debate whether a government depending on majority support would ever succeed, in a rich country, in transferring any substantial proportion of the national wealth to the minority who were poor. Nevertheless, I assume that this is an open question, that significant changes could occur within existing structures of government in response to the pressure of interest and ideas, and that it is therefore worth while to examine different ideologies and consider their implications for policy.

Attempts to define the poor and to account for their poverty are many and various, and explanations of poverty place different emphasis on individual character, the structure of society or, more recently, the idea of the so-called 'culture of poverty'. To analyse the response which governments make to problems of poverty and inequality I have chosen to distinguish three types of approach or three 'models' of welfare. Each is associated with different beliefs about the causes and nature of poverty, and each is based on different assumptions as to how national resources and opportunities should be distributed.

The attempt to identify different ways of approaching problems of social distribution does not, of course, imply that any country at any time has observed policies that fit neatly into one or other category. It is much more likely that different kinds of approach will be expressed in different pieces of mutually contradictory legislation existing side by side. The purpose of distinguishing between different strategies or objectives is not to describe or explain historical developments, but to point to the ideologies and principles which lie behind the policies and to clarify the practical implications of different beliefs.

The three approaches and their supporting ideologies are associated roughly with the political right, left and centre. The first, which I call 'laissez-faire', is based on a rather simple form of individualism. It puts great value on economic growth and maximising wealth and emphasises individual free choice in making contracts and agreements of all kinds.[2] The distribution of income and wealth, education, medical services and other forms of social care depends on the productive system and on individual bargaining power with a minimum of interference from the state either to protect the weak or to restrain the powerful. Poverty tends to be taken for granted as the lot of a large proportion of the population. It only becomes a matter for government action at the point at which living standards fall below the minimum for subsistence or threaten the rest of the community. In other words, this kind of approach is linked to an absolute rather than a relative conception of poverty. Second, and in contrast, is the 'socialist' approach, which stresses the value of equality and common rights to take part in political, social and economic activites. Individual freedom is similarly emphasised but differently interpreted; it is a matter of 'freedom to' rather than 'freedom

4

from'. The government becomes responsible for arranging the environment to permit everyone similar opportunities for making positive choices and to provide comparable standards of amenity, rather than limiting its activities to preventing acute destitution. Distribution is according to need so that in a perfectly working system poverty would not exist.

The third strategy can be described as 'liberal'.[3] It lies between the first two. It emphasises opportunity and individual freedom and attaches great importance to the market as a method of social distribution. At the same time, however, it admits government responsibility for guaranteeing minimum standards which are not determined by the essentials for subsistence but related to the living standards of the rest of the community.

A more detailed examination of the three concepts or approaches may help to distinguish them more clearly and to identify the different types of policy which they imply. The *laissez-faire* view is firmly based on two assumptions: a belief in the market as the fairest and most efficient means of determining standards of living and opportunities, and a commitment to the idea of individual freedom as a supreme value. The two assumptions have similar implications – that government intervention is dangerous and undesirable in so far as it interferes with the economic system or constrains the free choice of individuals. The proper functions of government, in this view, are to establish and maintain the conditions in which individuals can exercise their freedom and make their choices. This means above all attending to national security and internal order – responsibilities which cannot be carried out by individuals. It also means that the government steps in to act as a referee where interests clash, then withdraws again as quickly as possible when disputes are resolved.

The nature of the social policies which reflect such beliefs are fairly obvious. Government intervention is kept to the minimum to prevent starvation or to control environmental conditions which are so bad as to threaten health. The object is to encourage and persuade people to provide for themselves rather than to organise services which are run by the state; and persuasion works through a system of rewards and punishments rather than direct control, as the latter would infringe individual liberties. This kind of approach is very evident in some aspects of nineteenth-century British policy. The New Poor Law is a good example of a piece of legislation deliberately designed to offer only a minimum of support to the destitute. Its guiding principles of 'less eligibility' and 'deterrence' were to be made effective by stopping outdoor relief to the able-bodied and substituting maintenance in the workhouse where living standards were to be deliberately reduced below the level of the lowest-paid independent labourer.[4] And there were ad-

ditional penalties : families entering the workhouse were split up, sometimes inhabiting separate institutions though more commonly different
parts of the same building, and pauperism also automatically involved
the loss of voting rights.

The situation of the pauper was thus both unpleasant and shameful
and the offer of 'the house', the most obvious badge of pauper status,
was used as a convenient and automatic test of destitution. Only those
genuinely incapable of supporting themselves would, it was argued,
accept relief on such terms. The legislation was essentially a means for
dealing with 'voluntary unemployment', thought by the Poor Law Com-
missioners of 1832 to be the major cause of pauperism, and for ending
the practice of subsidising the low wages of men in work from the poor
rates. Thus the Poor Law avoided interfering either with the economy on
the one hand or individual independence on the other, by arranging
that even the worst-paid independent jobs should be preferable to
pauperism and so maintaining an incentive, if not an obligation, to
work.[5] The government was concerned only with the most acute destitution and then only if an application was made for poor relief. It was
not interested in the fact that the wages paid for independent work
might fail to maintain a family at a minimum subsistence level. Measures
to adjust employment incomes to needs through minimum-wage legislation or family allowances were not contemplated as a state responsibility, any more than a programme of cash grants as of right to maintain
those temporarily or permanently unable to work.

Associated with this kind of approach, where state intervention is
kept to a minimum, are certain assumptions both about the nature of
poverty and about its causes. In the first place, poverty tends to be
defined in terms of cash. The state of being poor or not poor depends
on the possession of a particular income. Following Rowntree and
Booth, the major social surveys of the first half of the twentieth century
in Britain have all used income as a measure of poverty, and it has been
a minimum income sufficient only for essential needs. It is interesting
that the authors of the Merseyside survey recognised the difficulty of
such a definition. A professional family, they observed, could not live
without serious discomfort on an income which a working-class family
would find extravagant,[6] but none of the theoretical problems raised by
this observation were examined. Rowntree, in his early York survey
though not in his later ones, distinguished between poverty due to
insufficient income and that due to mis-spending, but it is the failure to
attain a standard of life measurable in terms of the price of a range of
consumption goods that is at issue. Also, Rowntree clearly accepts
environmental circumstances, bad housing, poor amenities and lack of
education as causes of poverty but not, significantly, as in themselves
constituting poverty. Only those who could not or did not buy the

essentials for physical health were classified as poor. It is worth quoting Rowntree's own description of the physical-efficiency standard.

And let us clearly understand what 'mere physical efficiency' means. A family living upon the scale allowed for in this estimate must never spend a penny on railway fare or omnibus. They must never go to the country unless they walk. They must never purchase a half-penny newspaper or spend a penny to buy a ticket for a popular concert. They must write no letters to absent children, for they cannot afford to pay the postage. They must never contribute anything to their church or chapel, or give any help to a neighbour which costs them money. They cannot save nor can they join sick club or Trade Union because they cannot pay the necessary subscription. The children must have no pocket money for dolls, marbles or sweets. The father must smoke no tobacco, and must drink no beer. The mother must never buy any pretty clothes for herself or for her children, the character for the family wardrobe as for the family diet being governed by the regulation 'Nothing must be bought but that which is absolutely necessary for the maintenance of physical health, and what is bought must be of the plainest and the most economical description'. Should a child fall ill, it must be attended by the parish doctor; should it die, it must be buried by the parish. Finally, the wage-earner must never be absent from his work for a single day.

If any of these conditions are broken, the extra expenditure involved is met, *and can only be met*, by limiting the diet; or, in other words, by sacrificing physical efficiency.[7]

Secondly, there is a tendency, associated with the individualist approach, to look for the causes of poverty in personality or in circumstances beyond human control. The poor may be condemned as irresponsible, weak or wicked, but not necessarily, for it is admitted that poverty may also arise through misfortune. In so far as the misfortune results from a particular ordering of society, however, from a particular hierarchy of wealth and power, then it must be endured. Interference with the established social structure is regarded as impossible or undesirable or dangerous.

In the nineteenth century in Britain it was a major preoccupation of the Charity Organisation Society to distinguish the deserving from the undeserving poor; all appeals for charity were carefully investigated so that the appropriate help could be given to the former and the latter could be directed to the semi-penal Poor Law.[8] Help for the deserving consisted of small cash grants or services in kind or useful advice calculated to relieve the situation of the poor or strengthen them to bear it. But it was taken for granted that their condition was inevitable. There was little conception of poverty as a direct expression of the way in which society was organised and capable of being removed or alleviated by deliberate planning. Hence Mrs Webb's remark about the Charity Organisation Society that they 'had not got the faintest glimmer of what I have called "the consciousness of collective sin" '.[9]

The significance of this kind of attitude lies not so much in the moral character attributed to the poor but in the conception of poverty as a problem of the individual rather than of society. It is well expressed in the report of a district committee of the Charity Organisation Society for 1876.

> The principle is, that it is good for the poor that they should meet all the ordinary contingencies of life, relying not upon private or public charity, but upon their own industry and thrift, and upon the powers of self help that are to be developed by individual and collective effort. . . . The working man does not require to be told that temporary sickness is likely now and then to visit his household; that times of slackness will occasionally come; that if he marries early and has a large family, his resources will be taxed to the uttermost; that if he lives long enough, old age will render him more or less incapable of toil – all these are contingencies of a labourer's life, and if he is taught that as they arise they will be met by State relief or private charity he will assuredly make no effort to meet them himself. A spirit of dependence, fatal to all progress, will be engendered in him, he will not concern himself with the causes of his distress, or consider at all how the condition of his class may be improved; the road to idleness and drunkenness will be made easy to him, and it involves no prophesying to say that the last state of a population influenced after such a fashion will certainly be worse than the first. One thing there is which true charity does require the working man to be told, and it is the aim of this society to tell him, not in words merely, but in acts that cannot be confuted. We desire to tell him that those who are born to easier circumstances sympathise with the severe toil and self denial which his lot imposes upon him; that many are standing beside him ready and even eager to help if proper occasion should arise; and that if he, or wife, or child should be stricken with *protracted* sickness, or with some special infirmity, such as we all hope to escape, there are those at hand who will gladly minister to his necessities, and do their best at least to mitigate the suffering which it may be beyond their power to remove.[10]

Beliefs of this kind have obvious implications for public policies for dealing with poverty. Many members of the Charity Organisation Society opposed proposals for universal state pensions and other government welfare schemes because they considered indiscriminate public services were inevitably degrading and would undermine independence, thrift and self-help.

The Charity Organisation Society as such has disappeared, though it continues as the Family Welfare Association, but its concern to fight poverty through careful attention to individual cases lives on in the social-work profession. Few modern case workers would explicitly combine their preoccupation with individual cases with opposition to government reforms or deny the need to develop some public services on a universal basis. Nevertheless there is a potential conflict between the commitment to tackling individual problems through case work and a view which emphasises the environmental causes and nature of poverty. It is a conflict underlined by Professor Dudley Duncan when he asserts that 'poverty is not a trait but a condition'.[11]

This leads us to the socialist approach – fundamentally opposed to *laissez-faire* in insisting that the distribution of resources should be on the basis of need rather than ability to pay. The market system where supply is governed by effective demand is rejected because demand is regarded as quite different from need. Nor is so much importance attached to safeguarding individual freedom; commitment to the values of equality and fairness means that individual liberties may be increasingly challenged and increasingly limited. Similarly the moral virtues of independence and self-help are less emphasised, partly perhaps because opportunities for developing such qualities are reckoned to be largely a matter of social and economic circumstances.

The attempt to build a society where goods and services are distributed according to need is beset with enormous problems – conceptual as well as practical. First is that of defining, assessing and measuring need, of determining priorities, of deciding which needs are to be met and to what degree. Needs, of course, can be very variously interpreted. In a hierarchical society the needs of different groups for income or education may be accepted as very different; but the socialist does not admit such distinctions. Human beings share similar needs which are linked to opportunities for developing their personalities and abilities and which vary with mental and physical constitution but not with economic circumstances, 'the vulgar irrelevancies of class and income'. Socialists are inevitably concerned about inequalities in so far as those reflect not the natural differences between men but the way in which society is organised.

Such ideas have clear implications for government policies. They imply a degree of intervention by the state which far exceeds anything that would be contemplated by supporters of *laissez-faire*. Government activity goes beyond what may be necessary to guarantee a minimum, subsistence standard of living. It becomes the aim of public policies to ensure equal opportunities for a wide range of activities and experiences, and also to prevent great disparities in living standards which might result from differing ability to use opportunities.

Thus the measure of poverty used by the socialist is neither related to minimum needs nor expressed in terms of cash. Poverty is defined in relation to the lives of the rest of the community; and it is concerned with the quality of education, medical care, houses and the whole physical and social environment. Thus even the effective guarantee of an adequate income would be only a partial answer to the problem of poverty, for such a measure is essentially palliative. It may provide enough cash for a given standard of living, but it does little to improve the opportunities or experiences of the poor. It does not directly affect the poverty of physical, cultural and social environment which is often associated with financial poverty but which also exists independently.

Furthermore, the socialist is concerned with low living standards and poor environment for their own sake, regardless of whether they lead to or reflect some form of personal, social or economic disaster. He would tend to explain individual breakdown in terms of social structure and material circumstances, and he would be inclined to look for the remedy through changes in social institutions. Poverty is defined not so much as a matter of individual personality, individual choice or individual misfortune, but as a social phenomenon, a consequence of the way particular societies distribute opportunities and rewards. In industrial countries old people have little chance of employment and form a high proportion of the poor; men's wages are not adjusted to family size and large families are particularly vulnerable to poverty; modern industrial processes demand educated and skilled workers and the badly educated and unskilled figure largely among the poor.

Insistence that poverty is largely a reflection of the social structure suggests particular kinds of strategies for dealing with it which characteristically imply increasing government intervention in social and economic affairs. If the number of years a child spends in school and the qualifications he eventually receives are highly significant in keeping him out of poverty when he grows up, and are also as much a matter of social background as of natural ability, then a major attack on poverty could be the reform of the education service and training arrangements to provide the same opportunities for working-class children or negroes or immigrants – whoever constitute the poor – as for the children of middle-class parents. This kind of approach raises many more complex problems; it is no good educating more children if there are no suitable jobs for them and few chances for them to influence political decisions. Such a programme, if it is to avoid futility, personal frustration and political conflict, must involve substantial planning of the economy and substantial modification of the power structure. Nor can educational reform be accomplished entirely within the educational system; the material and cultural environment from which children come may have to be radically changed before high standards of achievement can be expected.

Policies to extend educational opportunities cannot of course be explained entirely in terms of a response to the threat of economic insecurity for the uneducated. Plans for educational expansion may also reflect the desire to increase national productivity, anxiety to appease popular agitation, or the belief in individual rights which is a second characteristic of the socialist position. Children, it is argued, have a right to be educated whatever their social status, and educational inequality between different social classes should be mitigated by deliberate public planning. In the same way arrangements for the distribution of medical services according to need rather than ability to pay may be an expression of a belief in equal rights as well as of a wish to avoid the damage to the economy or the individual poverty consequent on ill-health.

Such a conception of the status of the poor has very important implications for the organisation of social services. The emphasis on rights to a wide range and high standard of services regardless of the individual's capacity to buy them means that dependence on the state is less a matter for shame than a normal entitlement of everyday life.[12] In the nineteenth century the poor had a very clear status. It was the object of Poor Law policy to degrade the pauper, and that situation involved the sacrifice of both independence and respectability. By contrast the socialist conception emphasises rights to benefits and services and insists that applicants or claimants should be treated with consideration and respect. Rights for the poor, however, do not only mean the right to claim state assistance without stigma. They also mean the right to public services of a reasonable quality related to the standards available for those who support themselves, and according with the wishes of the people who use them rather than governed by the minimum subsistence principles of the Poor Law. This is an expression of respect for the poor. It implies a rejection of the idea that standards of living should be determined by individual economic power and an assertion that it is a proper function of the state to maintain adequate standards where individual effort fails.

The aim to distribute opportunities of various kinds more widely is an aspect of the more radical approach which sees financial poverty as only one element of a much larger problem. But poverty may be seen not only as lack of opportunity but as manifest in the immediate physical and social environment. Thus it can be defined geographically in terms of districts where a high proportion of the population is poor financially and also suffers from bad housing, an ugly and unhealthy environment, poor-quality public services and a lack of amenities of all kinds.

This geographical definition of poverty is now often linked with the idea of 'community development', which assumes that the problem of poor areas is a double one. It is partly a matter of improving public services but it is also, and perhaps this is a necessary first step, a matter of awakening local people to an awareness of their needs and rights and helping them to express and claim them. Once they have been made explicit, appropriate steps may then be taken for meeting community demands – pressure on the official bodies for new or extra services, some form of unofficial community action, or some joint endeavour of official and voluntary effort. The socialist would question the easy assumption that the needs of such districts could not be met by better public services, though at the same time he would welcome the attempt to encourage the formation and expression of popular opinion.

The third approach, the liberal one, is difficult to define clearly as it falls between the first two. It rejects the minimum subsistence standard as a satisfactory measure of poverty, but it also rejects egalitarian aims and ideals. It advocates a 'civilised' standard of living for those depending on state aid, but it is also anxious to limit state help to those who can be shown to be in need. The liberal accepts the market as an important determinant of living standards and attaches great importance to freedom of choice. He prefers individuals to be responsible and independent and to arrange privately for as high a standard of welfare as they individually choose or can afford.[13] The main job for the public services, in his view, is to guarantee a minimum standard for those who cannot support themselves. It is in this sense that the liberal accepts the market as a distributor of life-chances and opportunities. The essential common element in the *laissez-faire* and the liberal attitudes, and which distinguishes both from the socialist approach, is the readiness to allow a man's social and economic position to be determined by the wages he can earn or the wealth that he owns. Those who hold *laissez-faire* or liberal views see universal state provision as demoralising, as inefficient, as destructive of freedom of choice, as inviting abuse, and they therefore seek to restrict it to those who can demonstrate their need.

Such beliefs are much in evidence in the social policies of the industrial countries at the present time. In the rich nations there is a clear reluctance to accept further redistribution of income or a higher rate of public expenditure on welfare services. In 1968 Wilbur Cohen, the head of the United States Social Security Administration, submitted a plan to abolish poverty to the President's Commission on Income Maintenance Programs. He started by pointing out that poverty in the United States was no longer a matter of productive capacity. The country had sufficient resources to guarantee a continuing income for everyone – working or not – which would ensure a 'modest but adequate standard of living'. In speaking of the need for better assistance and security programmes, however, the first requirement he listed was a continued high rate of economic growth.[14] And it is common for the more prominent members of both Labour and Conservative parties in Britain to argue that increased public expenditure must be conditional on economic growth.[15] In other words, higher incomes or better services for the poor depend on a larger total national income rather than on modifying the existing distribution.

Income-maintenance programmes in Britain express the liberal approach clearly in limiting cash grants to a very low level. In 1942 Beveridge argued for a scheme which would produce a minimum income for everyone, those falling outside the defined insured categories were to be covered by public assistance and the families of men in work were to be supported by children's allowances. With some modification the idea of a minimum still forms the basis of the social-security scheme. Although the minimum has been redefined in so far as assistance and insurance scales have risen substantially more than prices since 1948, there is no evidence of greater equality between rich and poor. The relation of cash benefits to the current, average industrial wage remains much the same as in 1948.

In Britain the official minimum does in fact obtain widely, if not universally. In America attempts to define and provide a minimum living standard have been much less successful. The federal and state insurance and welfare programmes do not guarantee enough money to raise families from poverty, as it is officially defined by the Social Security Administration, and nor do families who are poor necessarily receive public assistance. In 1966 two-thirds of those receiving assistance remained poor, while only a quarter of the poor received public assistance.[16] In both countries private schemes supplement state benefits for those in particular occupations, and such arrangements are encouraged by exchequer subsidies or tax remission.

The belief in selective policies which restrict state help to people who can demonstrate their need, which is also fundamental to the liberal position, and the linked assumption that by and large a man's economic power should determine his living standards, are evident in many branches of British social policy. On the one hand, means tests of various kinds are widely and increasingly used to determine eligibility for benefits. Beveridge's plan for social security, where every insured person would receive an adequate income as of right and without any enquiry into resources when he was unable to work, has in fact been largely replaced by a system where the minimum is only available through public assistance which involves careful enquiry into circumstances and needs. Furthermore, the cost of services originally intended to be free to the consumer, or which were heavily subsidised by public money, has been increasingly shifted to the people who use them. This is true of the National Health Service, and it is also true of housing, or rather of those houses which are rented, whose tenants are to be expected to pay the full economic rent unless their income in relation to their needs falls below a nationally defined minimum. This is quite consistent with liberal doctrine; people should on the whole contribute to the services they use and should only be excused contributions if they are without the necessary resources.

At the same time as it is argued that state provision should be kept to a minimum, it is also suggested that those able to do so should be encouraged to buy better standards of provision privately and should be helped by being allowed to contract out of the public social services. The advocates of such policies support them for two reasons. First, they anticipate better-quality services as a result of increased competition and the abandoning of state monopoly provision and, second, they welcome the increased possibility for individuals to express their choices and preferences in education, health and pensions, for example. This kind of approach is expressed in the recent plans of the Conservative party in Britain for reforming social-security arrangements in such a way that pensions will be made up of two elements : a basic minimum payment guaranteed by the state and a supplement related to individual incomes arranged through private schemes for those who belong to them. Super-annuation has been a very controversial element in the social-security programme in Britain. Before the new Conservative proposals appeared the Labour party had already committed itself to a plan to relate pensions to individual earnings, so acknowledging that earnings capacity should determine rights to higher benefits[17] and rejecting the earlier Beveridge scheme which provided a universal flat rate of benefit related to needs rather than economic status.

The debate surrounding the choice of universal or selective social policies illustrates the division between the defender of *laissez-faire* at one extreme and the socialist at the other; the former is intent on limiting state provision both by restricting it to cases of proved need and in keeping the standards low; the latter is equally intent on extending services of high quality to the whole population. For the socialist, the commitment to universal services reflects not only the belief that this is the best way to make sure that the services will reach all who need them, and not only the belief in equality – that human beings have a range of educational and social needs which should be provided for without reference to their economic situation. It also expresses a more fundamental view about the way in which society should be organised : it is right and desirable that individuals should share common experiences and such sharing demonstrates and fosters a sense of mutual responsibility which is an essential foundation for social life.

Professor Titmuss, who was the major British spokesman for the socialist conception of welfare in the years after the last war, approaches the question of social integration in a different way when he argues that one of the most significant indications of an integrated society is the degree to which men and women are ready to offer gifts and services to others without any hope or expectation of return. He argues that the welfare society is dependent not so much on legislation as on the kind and quality of relationships that exist between its members, and it thus becomes a primary task of governments to avoid undermining and so far as possible to encourage people's feelings of mutual responsibility and concern. This raises important questions about the form that social policies and legislation should take, but they are questions which must await discussion until later chapters.

NOTES

1. Martin Rein, 'Problems in the Definition and the Measurement of Poverty', in *The Concept of Poverty,* ed. Peter Townsend (Heinemann, 1970).

2. See, for instance, Milton Friedman, *Capitalism and Freedom* (University of Chicago Press, 1962).

3. Labels can be misleading in this context where words change their meaning. Thus Professor Friedman argues that the true liberalism, in the historical sense, is expressed in the *laissez-faire* and individualistic doctrines of the nineteenth century, which he continues to champion. The enemies of liberalism, however, have stolen its clothes, and modern American (and British) 'liberals' support a degree of state intervention which would horrify their forebears. Nevertheless, with all its risks, I propose to label the three strategies or models (1) *laissez-faire,* (2) socialist and (3) liberal. I do not use the term 'conservative' for type (1), because, although associated with an absolute conception of poverty, the conservative tradition in Britain has not been *laissez-faire.*

4. In some cases adherence to the principle of deterrence led to conditions for paupers that were worse than those for convicted prisoners. S. and B. Webb, *English Poor Law History,* vol. 2, part 1 (Frank Cass, 1963) p. 391.

5. The need to keep public grants low to avoid reducing incentives to work and to refuse assistance to employed men altogether has been a primary preoccupation of social-security programmes. The proposals of the President's Commission on Income Maintenance Programs of 1969 to pay income supplements to men in employment is a significant assertion of the need for governments to interfere in the economy in order to support those actually working rather than limiting themselves to assisting those unable to work.

6. D. Caradog Jones (ed.), *The Social Survey of Merseyside,* vol 1 (Hodder & Stoughton, 1934) p. 149.

7. B. Seebohm Rowntree, *Poverty – A Study of Town Life* (Macmillan, 1901) p. 133.

8. See Charles Loch Mowat, *The Charity Organisation Society* (Methuen, 1961).

9. Beatrice Webb, *My Apprenticeship*, 2nd ed. (Longmans, Green, 1926) p. 177.

10. Quoted in Mowat, *The Charity Organisation Society*, p. 42.

11. Otis Dudley Duncan, 'Inheritance of Poverty or Inheritance of Race?', in *On Understanding Poverty*, ed. Daniel P. Moynihan (Basic Books, 1968) p. 88.

12. This is closely linked to the debate about the 'institutional' or 'residual' nature of social services. See Robert Pinker, *Social Theory and Social Policy* (Heinemann, 1971) chap. 3.

13. See the publications of the Institute of Economic Affairs for an example of this type of approach.

14. W. J. Cohen, 'A Ten-Point Program to Abolish Poverty', *Social Security Bulletin*, vol. 31, no. 12 (December 1968).

15. Those who question the assumed advantages of economic growth are in a tiny minority. But see E. J. Mishan, *Growth: the Price We Pay* (Staples Press, 1969), as well as J. K. Galbraith, *The Affluent Society* (Hamish Hamilton, 1958).

16. Molly Orshanski, 'The Shape of Poverty in 1966', *Social Security Bulletin*, vol. 31, no. 3 (March 1968).

17. And so performing in Professor George's words an 'ideological somersault'. Victor George, *Social Security and Society* (Routledge & Kegan Paul, 1973) p. 32.

CHAPTER 2

Kinship and Welfare

All societies have their own peculiar ways of allocating income, goods and services among their members. The pattern of the distribution which emerges in any particular case reflects many aspects of social structure. In this chapter I shall discuss some of the ways in which family structure and organisation influence the demand and need for various kinds of welfare services, bearing in mind the association of different types of family with different types of economy and, at the local community level, the way in which a particular occupation may affect family roles and relationships.

Economic growth brings with it widespread problems of material and social well-being. The rapid increase in urban populations creates a need for a range of public services and controls to protect health and safeguard amenities; and in later stages of economic development, movements out of town centres or to new areas of growth create fresh problems in the decaying 'inner rings' of the older cities which house shifting populations in poor material conditions and which are now becoming the typical problem areas of the highly industrialised countries.[1] Whatever the factors that influence the pattern of need or the distribution of welfare and of services, the average level of welfare which can be achieved within any country is limited by the total national wealth. On the whole, the wealthier countries tend to spend a larger proportion of their income on social-security services than do the poorer countries. However, if we consider only the wealthy group, the wealthiest devote a smaller proportion of their wealth to this end than other countries in the same group.[2]

Although a country's social policies are limited, however, they are not determined by its public resources. Even in the richest nations with the most developed policies, individual security and welfare may depend relatively little on state services. The family and the market may be more significant in determining living standards, though the relative importance of the various institutions, public and private, varies in different countries. Wealth and status may be largely a result of family position, a situation into which an individual is born and from which it

17

is unlikely that he will move very far. They may, however, be less a matter of ascription and more a result of achievement where family influence becomes less important in the face of publicly devised methods to enable individuals to gain for themselves jobs and incomes which depend on personal abilities and accomplishments. Advanced education may be virtually restricted to children whose parents have the money to pay for it or who are able to use the educational institutions to their own advantage. Alternatively, the criterion for admission to colleges and universities may be a child's measured intelligence or even his desire for some kind of further training. In other words, the availability of education may be determined by private wealth and family resources, or it may be publicly and bureaucratically controlled in relation to defined characteristics. Not that the family, as long as it remains a social unit for bringing up children, can ever be robbed of all influence in favour of an entirely impartial selection procedure. Family circumstances are an important component in a child's intelligence and may have an adverse or favourable effect on his achievement, his measured ability, his chances of further education and subsequently of highly paid, secure or agreeable occupation.

A high degree of industrialisation tends to be associated with a particular kind of family structure. This is not necessarily a causal connection. Knowledge is too incomplete to allow certain generalisations about the effects of industrial development on family organisation. It has been argued that the process may work the other way in that a particular kind of family structure may encourage industrial growth. But whatever the case, there is indisputably a 'fit', as Goode puts it,[3] between industrial society and the nuclear family and the two, in fact, tend to occur together. In the development of social policies the proper division of responsibility between public bodies, private organisations and the family has been a matter for continual debate, and it is therefore important to see how the combination of industrial society and the nuclear family affects the need for public services. The family is essential in supplying care, support and security, but its ability to do this varies both with its structure and with the different social contexts in which it exists.

At one extreme is the extended family where three or more generations may share a household or live closely grouped together, and where elaborate rules of conduct govern the way in which individuals standing in a given relationship shall behave to one another and the kinds of services or support they are entitled to expect. This kind of organisation is generally found in the poor countries where industrialisation has not begun. In contrast is the nuclear family of married couple and dependent children, which usually forms a household unit in the advanced industrial societies. Ties of duty or affection with a much wider group of persons are, of course, recognised and maintained and, where geography and communications permit, regular, mutual exchanges of services may be common. But separate dwellings are generally preferred, and where sharing occurs it tends to be in response to some specific social or economic need – handicap, old age or housing shortage.

In various ways the extended family is in a position to provide more effective care and support for its members. To some extent this is a matter of its actual structure, the presence of a comparatively large number of adults who can act as substitutes for one another or at any rate share responsibilities in the care of children or old people, for example. But it is also a matter of the wider environment. The extended family tends to exist within the more primitive economies where scientific knowledge is scarce or non-existent, where methods and techniques of production are simple, and where there is little specialisation or division of labour. In these circumstances the family can operate as an educational institution where the older members pass on to the younger ones the traditional skill and knowledge appropriate, in view of their sex and family position, for the tasks which they will later perform.

This educative role which the family plays in undeveloped societies is fully demonstrated in anthropological writing. It also occurs in more familiar places where, for certain groups, the economic structure is such that a child's future is more or less decided at birth. Arensberg and Kimball illustrate this kind of situation in Ireland, County Clare, in the mid-1930s. The training children received within their families was designed for two things : to fit them for their future position within the families they would form and to prepare them for their tasks within an agricultural economy.

> The division of labour between the sexes arises within a field of larger interests and obligations. It is part of the behaviour expected reciprocally of husband and wife. It is a functional element of their relationship within the family.
>
> The training each sex receives from childhood in farm work reflects this fact. Each learns his or her part in farm economy, not as a vocational preparation but as a making ready for marriage. The boy acquires his man's skills and techniques for the farm and farm family he may head himself some day ; the girl learns the woman's role as an integral part of her future state of wife and mother.[4]

Farm-work was divided according to sex, lighter jobs on the whole going to the women, but there was also a division of labour by age. Arensberg and Kimball speak of the father as director and owner of the farm on which even adult sons worked under supervision and to whom necessary decisions were referred. They continue to describe the situation of the growing child.

> He forms part of the productive unit which is his own family. The techniques of farming are passed on to him, and he learns them under the direction of his father, uncles and brothers. At their hands he acquires the conditioning which will fit him to form a farm family of his own, thus to continue the traditional pattern. Naturally, his conditioning is more than merely technological; he gets on the farm the full training which makes him a member of his class and time.[5]

Instances of family training occur even within an industrialised economy and when the family ceases to be a productive unit. Young and Willmott point to the persistence of this tradition among certain groups of workers in Bethnal Green – particularly among those, such as dockers, with high prestige and strong traditions. 'The son was the father's mate. He carried his son while he was learning and the sons later on carried their fathers when they were old.'[6]

In many ways, simple productive systems can accommodate to individual capacities and so ease the job of the extended family in the support of persons who might otherwise be entirely dependent. Where the work group depends for its livelihood on a wide range of tasks demanding varying degrees of strength or agility or concentration it is possible to adjust work to the powers of individuals in a way which is much more difficult in a highly specialised economy based on elaborate technology. The mentally and physically handicapped can more easily take some part in agricultural work than in the more demanding occupations characteristic of industrial society, and a fixed retirement age at which men must leave paid employment does not occur in the traditional societies.[7] Men stop working when they become unfit, and even then they may find less exacting jobs among the variety of tasks which have to be carried out.

> Old men among the Hopi tend their flocks until feeble and nearly blind. When they can no longer follow the herd, they work on in their fields and orchards, frequently lying down on the ground to rest. They also make shorter and shorter trips to gather herbs, roots, and fuel. When unable to go to the fields any longer they sit in the house or Kiva where they card and spin, knit, weave blankets, carve wood, or make sandals. Some continue to spin when they are blind or unable to walk, and it is a common saying that 'an old man can spin to the end of his life'. Corn shelling is women's work but men will do it, especially in their dotage. Old women will cultivate their garden patches until very feeble and 'carry wood and water as long

as they are able to move their legs'. They prepare milling stones, weave baskets and plaques out of rabbit weed, make pots and bowls from clay, grind corn, darn old clothes, care for children, and guard the house; and when there is nothing else to do, they will sit out in the sun and watch the drying fruit. The old frequently express the desire to 'keep on working' until they die.[8]

Such opportunities for useful activity continuing into old age contrast with the enforced idleness which is often the lot of the majority of old people in industrial countries.

The quality of the care and support which the extended family affords in simple societies may, of course, be very low. It may educate its children, but often in only primitive techniques; it may care for the unemployed or the unemployable, the aged and the sick, but often at a level which barely reaches subsistence; and in the most extreme cases the pressure of economic circumstances can lead to the killing or abandoning of old people or children in order to protect the living standards of the rest of the group. Nevertheless, the possibilities of support which the extended family can offer in favourable circumstances are severely limited in the nuclear family, though here again the restricted functions are not only a reflection of family structure but also of the nature of the wider society in which the nuclear family tends to be found.

Comparatively small households are less dependable as institutions for caring for their members. The incapacity of either adult may mean that the family can no longer function as an economic or social unit and that children have to be dispersed to friends or relations or the public services. Similarly, the habit of independent living makes the care of old people less certain. In some communities the different generations, though living separately, may yet be near enough to supply many mutual services and it has been demonstrated that old people rely much more on their families for social support than on public provision.[9] Nevertheless, the partial exclusion from a wider residential family unit is bound to increase the need of old people for alternative forms of care.

The nuclear family, however, is a variable institution. Its organisation, the responsibilities of its members, and the relationships between them and between family and more distant relatives, vary with the character and the occupational structure of the local community, how far it is settled and integrated, whether it is rich or poor. The more 'privatised' the family, the more cut off from the local community or wider family network, the more vulnerable it becomes in times of crisis and the more likely to make demands on the public services.

Two very different kinds of family organisation are described by

Dennis, Henriques and Slaughter in their study of a Yorkshire mining town[10] and by Goldthorpe and his colleagues in their study of Luton.[11] In both cases family structure is related by the authors to geographical isolation, poverty and occupation. In the mining town a long tradition of bad relations between workers and employers in the pits and the common experience the miners shared of hard and dangerous work from which women were totally excluded both helped to produce a high degree of solidarity and companionship among the men, which was associated with marked separation of the lives of men and women. For the men both work and leisure activities were carried on outside their families. The women's responsibilities were, by contrast, housework and children and neither domestic tasks nor leisure were commonly shared with their husbands. Women had little expectation of nor opportunity for professional or social interests outside their homes; what social activities they had took place within the circle of neighbours and female relations. The domestic responsibilities of the men were largely confined to handing over part of their earnings to their wives as 'wages'.

The authors of *Coal Is Our Life* comment that the narrowness of outlook among the women in Ashton induced by their own social position in the mining community, itself socially isolated and inbred, seriously impaired their effectiveness in their main job – the bringing up of children. Nevertheless, the ready availability of female friends and relatives, and in particular the advice and support that daughters received from their mothers, eased the job of child care in a way which cannot happen in more self-contained family units like those of Luton.

In Luton, a comparatively recent settlement, family structure was in marked contrast to the pattern in Ashton. The lives of men and women were far less separate. Men shared domestic jobs and the care of children as well as leisure activities with their wives; and such activities tended to be centred on the home. The relatively high wages and the leisure time that the car workers could earn were used to provide security and comfort and amusement for their families rather than being spent on activities shared almost exclusively with male colleagues. The authors see this as associated with a shift away from more traditional working-class values towards the idea of a 'companionate' marriage: 'primacy was clearly given to the material well-being, the social cohesiveness and the autonomy of the conjugal family over against the demands or attractions of wider kinship or community ties'.[12] Moreover, although many Luton people were out of reach of their families for casual visiting and the exchange of services, they had not developed a pattern of neighbourly visiting which might have provided an alternative system of support. This would seem to be easily explained by shorter settlement and greater mobility, but the authors also link the 'privatisation' of family life to the occupational structure. The traditional bitter hostility which marked the relations between employers and employees in the mining town and the physical danger of work in the pits, which together helped to bind the men into a community from which women were excluded, were both absent in the motor industry.

Neither the Luton study nor *Coal Is Our Life* contain explicit attempts to analyse the effects of the different types of family structure on the demand for or use of public services. But the small family group in Luton existing independently of any more extensive network of support, supplied in Ashton by neighbours and relatives, seems inevitably more vulnerable in times of crisis.

Apart from the inherent weaknesses of the nuclear family, the nature of the advanced industrial societies in which it is commonly found emphasises in many ways the comparative fragility of such an institution in catering for the support of its members. It is a characteristic of rich countries that industrial processes and, indeed, professional occupations become increasingly based on an elaborate body of technological and scientific knowledge which is constantly changing. Jobs become more specialised and those who are to perform them require a high degree of technical competence. This affects the family's role in a number of ways. First, it cannot undertake the formal training of children for their future occupations, for training is no longer a matter of handing on traditional and general skills which are then applied in traditional ways by younger men. New techniques and skills have to be learned as advances in science and technology permit new methods of production, and the knowledge and experience which older people possess may often be irrelevant for younger people. Furthermore, given the variety of jobs which exist in an industrial country, no family group could possibly contain within itself the range of knowledge to give adequate instruction to its young members. So training becomes more and more the job of specialised public and private agencies operating independently of the kin group.

Second, the family loses some degree of control over the employment opportunities of its members. It is characteristic of modern industrial societies that employment increasingly depends on the possession of qualifications awarded by educational and professional bodies. Selection for different kinds of jobs becomes less a matter of family situation and more a matter for formal training and personal suitability. The efficiency of industrial, political and economic organisations must be safeguarded by insisting that those who work within them have the appropriate qualifications.

Increases in scientific knowledge and in specialisation have implications for family functions which go beyond education and employment. The growth of medical science, for example, means that medical care is no longer based on traditional remedies and folk-lore passed on and applied within the kin group. The practice of medicine becomes confined to a profession or number of professions with strict rules of membership and where services are organised outside the family on a governmental or private basis. More recently, interest has increased in the growth and development of young children, and professional and semi-professional groups have sprung up claiming an expert knowledge in various aspects of child care which challenges more traditional child-rearing practices and in this way further undermines family responsibility.

In such ways the family loses both power and authority. The younger members, to the extent that they depend less on their elders for material benefits, may also be less submissive to control. This would be consistent with families being more scattered geographically and with younger people feeling less obligation to look after older relatives, whose support would tend to become more a matter for agencies outside the family.[13] At the same time, public opinion about the proper limits of parental power over children alters and with it the possibilities of public interference to control parental behaviour and in extreme cases remove children from their families. Over the past hundred years in Great Britain, parental responsibility for the education and general care of young children has been defined in such a way as increasingly to limit the possibilities of parental choice: or, to put it another way, public agencies have assumed greater control over matters previously left to family discretion.

An obvious hazard which industrialisation brings is the added risk of dependency of various kinds. It is not only that the nuclear family may be less able and have less incentive to support old people, but the actual need for support is intensified in an industrial economy where there is a relatively rigid retirement age when a man must leave paid employment without having any alternative occupation. The loss of income, status and occupation which follow combine to produce a situation which is extremely difficult for the nuclear family to handle. But work in industrial economies involves other less foreseeable risks: the threat of unemployment resulting from structural changes or depression, and of redundancy where technological change makes particular methods of production and particular skills obsolete. Both situations lead to loss of earnings so that other means of support have to be found, and the weakness of the nuclear family from this point of view tends to mean that responsibility shifts to outside bodies. Individual firms or organisations may make quite comprehensive provision for their workers through sickness and pension schemes, arrangements for medical care, and so on. A variety of private profit-making bodies and charitable organisations supply health services, education, homes for the old and for children, and organise insurance against specified risks. And, finally, governments develop schemes of income maintenance and health and social care.

Another aspect of industrial economies is their need for a mobile labour force. As particular industries decline or grow, workers have to follow the available jobs, and highly trained persons – professionals, businessmen or civil servants – will generally have to leave their homes to find work. Where this kind of movement occurs, the nuclear family is clearly convenient. However, the ties with relatives other than man and wife or parents and children are weakened. Mutual services and close personal and social relationships are undermined by geographical distance.

Social as well as geographical mobility is a significant feature of industrialised nations. The need for a highly skilled labour force and for elaborate training for the increasing number of professional occupations, tends to lead to more democratic education systems with more or less serious efforts to enable clever children from all classes to have whatever education they can profit by. But education for children from poor homes may mean an introduction to a quite different set of values, as well as leading to more highly paid occupations which permit a different standard of living from that of the family of origin. So the possibility of conflict arises between a child and its parents and between brothers and sisters, as those who are chosen for a particular kind of education adopt new styles of life. Social as well as geographical separation can in this way undermine the bases of family solidarity.[14]

Thus, while the nuclear family in one sense fits the conditions and requirements of advanced industrial economies, it is at the same time a very inadequate institution for meeting the risks which such economies make more acute. The growth of scientific knowledge tends to rob the family of functions and powers which previously helped to keep it together and to maintain its authority, even though there are some modern inventions, such as television and the motor car, which seem to work in the other direction in providing joint activities which families share.

None the less, if family power and responsibility tend to decline in industrialised countries as more services come to be provided by the public authorities or outside private bodies, this is not equally true for all social groups. The rich, although they provide neither formal education nor training for their children, are still often able to buy privately higher-quality services than the state supplies, and to override the bureaucratic selection process which might otherwise exclude their children from the kind of education they desired. The same is true of medical services where it is possible to buy a higher standard of care privately. Moreover, although the rich must move about in search of jobs, they are better able to maintain family ties over wide distances. Poor families by contrast tend to have far less influence over the destinies of their children. Lack of resources means that they are obliged to depend on public services of whatever quality, and in practice the public services offered to the poor are frequently of a lower standard than those that are offered to the rich. In addition, the poor often lack the sophistication or knowledge to get full benefit from whatever provision may be available.

In other words, although in industrial societies public and private services organised outside the family may take over certain functions which in simpler societies are the responsibility of the family or kin group, the family still remains extremely resistant to the influence of public provision. The impact of outside services is always mediated through the family and modified by its particular culture. This is obvious enough at the upper end of the social structure where it is possible to choose whether or not to use public services. It is also obvious at the bottom of the hierarchy where the knowledge, capacity, persistence or confidence to make the best use even of what is provided is often missing. This situation has also its more positive side in that the public services may be deliberately rejected in favour of traditional practices. Young and Willmott pointed out in 1962 that many young women in Bethnal Green preferred to observe their mothers' views on child-rearing rather than the advice of visitors from the local health department.

There are, of course, particular kinds of family unit which are especially likely to be dependent, economically at any rate, on public services. Most important are the retired households: over two-thirds of old people in Great Britain rely on state grants of one sort or another as their main source of income though, by contrast, the social care of old people seems to be still more a family than a public affair. Families headed by women, or with only one parent in the household, are a second vulnerable group, and third are those with a large number of dependent children.

Family structure and industrial organisation are thus highly signifi-cant in determining the need for and distribution of goods and services of various kinds. Public services are likely to be most needed by particular kinds of family, by those where the head is unable to work, those that are incomplete and those with many dependants. They are also likely to be most needed in particular kinds of community. The long-established, stable communities such as are, or were, found in Bethnal Green, in the mining districts of England and Wales, and in some country areas where families and individuals are bound together by kinship, common residence and often common occupation, develop elaborate 'private' welfare systems based on mutual help and support and are often relatively independent of and resistant to public services. This may, of course, have its pathological aspects, as shown in the delinquent sub-culture in Liverpool described by J. B. Mays.[15] In contrast are the areas characterised by high mobility, which provide a home for people from very different backgrounds, often different countries, who have moved out of range of the influence, authority or support of their family group. It is in such areas, often in the decaying centres of the large industrial towns, sometimes in the relatively hygienic and carefully planned public housing estates of the pre- and post-war years, where high rates of delinquency, illegitimacy, family breakdown and other social problems reflect the lack of cohesion and social control, that the need for public systems of discipline, support and care are particularly obvious.

NOTES

1. This is a generalisation about Western countries. In Latin America and in Africa urbanisation has usually meant the growth of slums and 'shanty towns' on the outskirts of existing towns and cities.

2. Felix Paukert, 'Social Security and Income Redistribution : Comparative Experience', in U.S. Department of Health, Education and Welfare, *The Role of Social Security in Economic Development* (United States Government Printing Office, 1968) pp. 107–8. The figures refer to 1963.

3. William J. Goode, *World Revolution and Family Patterns* (Free Press, 1963).

4. Conrad M. Arensberg and Solan T. Kimball, *The Family and Community in Ireland* (Harvard University Press, 1948) p. 48.

5. Ibid. p. 51.

6. Michael Young and Peter Willmott, *Family and Kinship in East London* (Pelican, 1962) p. 98.

7. In his study of Malay fishermen, Professor Firth found that roughly half the men over sixty were still working, though at jobs which required relatively little effort. Raymond Firth, *Malay Fishermen : Their Peasant Economy* (Kegan Paul, Trench, Trubner & Co., 1946).

8. Leo William Simmons, 'Social Participation of the Aged in Different Cultures', in *Comparative Social Problems*, ed. S. N. Eisenstadt (Free Press, 1964) p. 180.

9. Ethel Shanas *et al.*, *Old People in Three Industrial Societies* (Routledge & Kegan Paul, 1968).

10. Norman Dennis, Fernando Henriques and Clifford Slaughter, *Coal Is Our Life* (Eyre & Spottiswoode, 1956).

11. John H. Goldthorpe *et al.*, *The Affluent Worker in the Class Structure* (Cambridge University Press, 1969).

12. Ibid. p. 108.

13. The situation of old people is also greatly affected by demo-

graphic trends. The drop in the birth rate, which continued during the first half of this century in Britain, and the rather later increase in the marriage rate has meant fewer children and fewer single women available to care for their parents.

14. Neil J. Smelser, *The Sociology of Economic Life* (Prentice-Hall, 1963).

15. J. B. Mays, *Growing Up in the City* (Liverpool University Press, 1954).

CHAPTER 3

Stratification and Welfare

The simplest forms of government intervention to tackle poverty are directed at avoiding hunger and disease. In the advanced industrial countries with which studies of social policy and administration are generally concerned, however, poverty has a special meaning. It is not the poverty of the undeveloped agricultural countries where the majority of the population is engaged in a constant struggle for survival, where malnutrition and disease are widespread, where medical and welfare services are grossly inadequate and where, in any case, economic development may claim a major share of national resources. It is rather a matter of distribution; of poverty which arises through inequality. If wealth were more evenly spread poverty could be eliminated. In the United States in 1969, for instance, 13 per cent of the total population were living below the adequacy level and it would have cost $9 billion to raise them out of poverty,[1] but since the last war the G.N.P. in the United States has increased on average by $16 billion annually (at 1966 prices) – a growth rate of roughly 2 per cent.

It is inequalities which give rise to the social problems confronting the industrialised countries. Poverty, in the sense of a standard of living too low to maintain health, has ceased to be a problem because total national wealth would be adequate to keep everyone above subsistence level if it were used to that purpose. And by and large the rich countries do contrive to prevent people from starving, though incomplete provision or faulty administration may perpetuate severe hardship. Poverty may be defined, however, as a relative state, so that to be poor depends on the relationship between an individual or group and what is normal for the country they live in, rather than on failure to reach a standard sufficient to provide the necessities for subsistence.[2]

Comparing nations of different levels of wealth and industrial development, inequalities of income and of standards of living are greatest within the poorer and less developed countries. Here a large proportion of the population lives at a standard bordering on or below physical subsistence – a degree of material hardship experienced by only a very small minority in the rich countries. At the same time, the resources of the underdeveloped countries are hopelessly inadequate for dealing with the intractable problems of endemic disease and poverty which face them. A comparison of real income per head, based on an index taking the United States as a hundred, shows the United Kingdom with real income per head of 59 and Ceylon and Ghana each with 4 in 1960.[3] During 1960 the United States spent 7 per cent of G.N.P. on social security,[4] the United Kingdom 11 per cent, Ceylon 4 per cent, and Ghana 1 per cent.[5] The infant mortality rate, a common index of the health of populations and of the need for social and medical care, varied between 12 in Sweden in 1969 and 20 in the United States in 1970, to 50 in Ceylon in 1968, and 168 in rural Turkey in 1967.[6] In 1970 the rich countries had one doctor for every 600 or 700 inhabitants, Turkey one for every 2000, and Ghana one for every 12,000 people[7] (see Table 3.1, p. 31).

However, it is a paradox that the very economic growth which produces the means to overcome the most acute poverty may intensify problems of inequality. Technological advance brings new methods of production and greater mechanisation; industries decline or move to new areas, leaving behind them redundancy and unemployment. Professor Meade argues that as countries grow richer it is perfectly possible for the distribution of income within them to become more unequal. He has in mind particularly what may happen in certain circumstances when industrial methods become more capital intensive.

> In the highly industrialised countries a substantial proportion of the real product does accrue to the owners of property and property is very unequally owned. There is already, therefore, a problem. The pattern of real wage rates which is required on efficiency grounds may lead to a very high level of real income per head for the small concentrated number of rich property owners. And it is possible, though not certain, that this problem will become more acute as a result of automation.[8]

Thus a higher proportion of the national income goes to investment and less to wages, and workers are competing for a smaller share of the national income.

It is usual to distinguish three aspects of inequality relating to income or wealth, status and power. In practice, advantage with respect to any of these attributes tends to be associated with similar advantages with regard to the others, but the connection is not a necessary one. Stratification systems influence both the supply of public welfare and the demand. Government social policies in democratic countries are not the outcome solely of pure reason, disinterested benevolence, or indeed of the exploitative machinations of some uniquely powerful group. They

TABLE 3.1

International comparisons: G.N.P. per head; real private consumption per head; expenditure on social security;
infant-mortality rates and proportion of doctors to population

Country	Real G.N.P. per head Index U.S.A. = 100, 1960	Real private consumption per head Index U.S.A. = 100, 1960	Expenditure on social security % G.N.P. 1960 or 1961	Expenditure on social security % G.N.P. 1965 or 1966	Infant mortality 1970	Population per doctor 1970 or 1971
U.S.A.	100	100	7·0	7·2	19·8	645
Sweden	81·4	77·4	11·7	15·6	11·7 (1969)	734 (1969)
Canada	69·6	77	9·6	9·6	18·8	684 (1969)
Australia	61·7	65·4	8·5	8·2	17·9	847 (1969)
U.K.	58·5	61·7	11·2	12·6	18·4	787 (England and Wales)
Denmark	58·1	59·2	10·8	13·2	14·2	704 (1968)
Germany (Fed. Rep.)	60·1	56·1	15·9	17·4	23·6	561
Portugal	13·8	17·0	4·7	5·3	58·0	1064
Yugoslavia	–	13·5	12·1	12·3	55·2	938
Turkey	7·7	9·8	1·5	1·7	168 (rural Turkey 1967)	2187
Ceylon	4·4	5·3	3·5	3·6	50·3 (1968)	–
Ghana	4·1	4·8	0·8	1·3	66·9[a] (1969)	12,392
Thailand	3·2	3·7	–	–	26·2[a] (1969)	7927

[a] Figures incomplete and unreliable.

SOURCES: Wilfred Beckerman, *International Comparisons of Real Incomes* (O.E.C.D., 1966); International Labour Office, *The Cost of Social Security 1964–6* (Geneva, 1972); United Nations, *Demographic Yearbook 1971* (New York, 1972) and *Statistical Yearbook 1972* (New York, 1973).

are a response to the varying pressures of different interests, and the balance of power and thus the pattern of welfare provision shifts through time. This is not to deny that stratification systems may themselves be modified by governments acting in accord with some kind of ideological commitment. But hierarchies of power and advantage are very resistant to change, as may be seen in the persistence of poverty and gross inequalities in Britain over the period since the Second World War, when both main political parties have been more or less committed to the idea of the welfare state. The Labour party in particular has claimed egalitarian objectives, but it has been largely ineffectual in significantly altering the existing distributions.

Race is a further important factor in stratification. The ethnic group to which a man belongs may impose inescapable limitations on his economic, social and political opportunities. In the most extreme cases apartheid policies may be supported by law. In apparently more tolerant societies, the legal or official extension of citizenship rights to all may none the less be undermined in practice by very wide differences in the quality of services and in the extent of opportunities available to different racial and ethnic groups, and by various forms of discrimination practised towards such minorities. Legislation which sets out to suppress overt discrimination is only a small and rather negative step towards removing the disadvantages and the handicaps which coloured people face in societies dominated by white men.

It is clear that a man's position in the stratification system will influence his need for and use of public social services. First, high income, whether derived from capital or earnings, is of extreme importance. Services can be bought which are of better quality than those provided through the public-welfare system. This is true in medicine, housing and education, to give only the most obvious examples. It has a special significance in the latter, for 'good' education opens up possibilities of jobs with high status, high salaries, and opportunities for exercising power, which are less accessible to the worse educated and not accessible at all to those who lack both education and social position.

High income and high status are not necessarily combined, though they often reinforce one another and either may be a means of achieving the other. Even where income is not large enough to allow private education or private medical treatment, middle-class families tend to get more benefit from the public services than the poor. Middle-class children frequently go to better schools than working-class children, stay longer and are more likely to proceed to higher education; more middle-class than working-class women are confined in hospitals. The reasons for such a situation are complex. It is partly a matter of geography: the middle classes and the working classes tend to live apart and for various reasons the schools and hospitals serving working-class areas are likely to be poorer than those serving middle-class areas. It is partly a matter of culture and values : middle-class values reinforce the education that children receive in schools and middle-class people are more at ease with professionals such as doctors and teachers. Finally, it is partly a matter of awareness of rights and the ability, knowledge and confidence to handle public bureaucracies.

The third element in stratification is political power which is, of course, closely associated with wealth and status. The failure of the poor to exercise their political rights has become a matter for debate both in the United States and in Britain, because it is particularly significant in relation to public social policy. The American 'war on poverty' has emphasised the need to awaken political consciousness among deprived and depressed communities and to involve local people in the planning of their own welfare programmes. In Britain there are numerous experiments, often initiated in the first instance at any rate by voluntary effort, which aim to inform people of their rights and encourage them to claim them. There are also more direct attempts to arouse political consciousness and activity. Community workers of many kinds, and not only voluntary workers, try to encourage local people to define and express their needs and to find ways of bringing local opinion to bear on decision-makers in the interests of better public services. The Community Development Projects in Britain are government-supported experiments which have such aims in view, though they attempt also to evaluate the effectiveness of various measures to raise the quality of life in poor areas.[9] This kind of intervention starts with the idea that improvement can be brought about in such depressed districts with the minimum of extra resources, by concentrating on fully co-ordinated public services and easy communication between public officials and local population so that welfare organisations are responsive and sensitive to local needs; and it emphasises the importance of articulate and informed public opinion. Such a strategy, if successful, implies a redistribution of political power and a consequent redirection of public welfare policies. No such redirection could be achieved, however, without a very large increase in spending in the public sector, and it is unclear how far it would be possible to introduce such radical policies without major political conflict.[10]

The analysis of stratification in terms of class, status and power is familiar enough to need little elaboration, but the significance of race and ethnicity is perhaps less widely recognised, even though it is becoming increasingly obvious in relation to public welfare services, so I propose to look at some aspects of the situation of some minority racial groups in more detail.[11]

The importance of colour, even in those countries which disclaim or have rejected official discriminatory policies, is evident enough. In the United States the levels of income, health and education of negroes are well below those of whites. What is more, Professor Duncan has shown that the income gap between negroes and whites is only partly explained by negro–white differences in such things as education and occupation of head of the household of origin, number of siblings, and education and occupation of the person concerned. The total income gap is $3790. Differences in family background account for $940, in family size for $70, in education for $520, and in occupation for $830. This leaves $1430, or rather over a third of the gap unexplained. As Duncan remarks, 'Unless and until we can find other explanations for it, this must stand as an estimate of income discrimination . . . .'[12] Another significant point to emerge from Duncan's analysis is that the statistical relation among variables is almost always weaker for negroes than for whites. Family background has a less certain influence on income for negroes than for whites; or, in other words, a favourable family background is a lesser advantage to a negro than to a white in terms of its association with occupational achievement or high income.

In Britain the handicaps imposed by race, particularly by colour, and those which result from immigration tend to mingle, though they are fairly easily separable. There is ample evidence that coloured people experience discrimination or show to less advantage in comparison with the white population in a wide variety of circumstances, in their search for work, in attempts to find houses and in education. Employment seems to be the area in which race, or at any rate a coloured skin, is associated with the most serious disadvantages. The relative economic status of different immigrant groups in Great Britain as revealed in the 1966 census shows 50 per cent of men from the Caribbean in manual occupations compared with 40 per cent of the total population, 36 per cent of Indians, 50 per cent of Pakistanis and 47 per cent of men from the Irish Republic. At the other end of the scale, 14 per cent of the total population were classified as employers, managers or professional workers compared with 2 per cent of men from the Caribbean, 8 per cent of those from the Irish Republic, 17 per cent of Indians and 6 per cent of Pakistanis.[13] Caribbean immigrants are particularly badly represented in the higher social groups compared with the total population and with other immigrants. They are over-represented in the lowest groups compared with the total population, though to an only slightly higher degree than Pakistanis. Such a distribution shows particular groups to be disproportionately concentrated in manual work and demonstrates that membership of these groups carries with it relatively poor chances of more highly paid and secure jobs; it does not necessarily imply discrimination, for the minority groups may lack the skill or qualifications to compete for more rewarding types of employment. But although differences in education and training may account to some extent for the concentration of Caribbean and Pakistani immigrants in the poorer jobs, this is only a partial explanation. It has been demonstrated that there is widespread discrimination in Britain, that the West Indians suffer most and that there is a tendency for experience of discrimination to be more widespread among the most highly qualified.[14]

Race also significantly affects the chances of renting or buying houses. The Political and Economic Planning Report summarised by Daniel and referred to above found that discrimination in housing created problems for West Indians second only to those arising out of poor employment prospects, but that Asians did not feel such discrimination so keenly. As part of the effort to discover the extent of discrimination, the P.E.P. enquiry arranged various 'situational tests'. In one of these, three 'testers' – a West Indian, a Hungarian and an Englishman – applied for accommodation in a selected number of cases where advertisements did not exclude coloured people. The three men claimed similar economic and social status but the West Indian experienced discrimination in over two-thirds of the applications, mostly being told that accommodation was already taken and, less often, being asked for a higher rent.[15]

Discrimination also occurred in attempts to buy houses where situational tests showed that the West Indian was treated differently from the Hungarian and the Englishman. The conclusions of the P.E.P. Report are an ominous warning about the future of race relations in Britain. 'In the sector we studied . . . there is racial discrimination varying from the massive to the substantial. The experience of white immigrants . . . compared to black or brown immigrants . . . leaves no doubt that the major component in the discrimination is colour.'[16]

There is evidence that in Britain prejudice against West Indians is greater than against Asians, but the amount of discrimination they encounter and their vulnerability to it is also partly determined by the immigrants themselves, by the strength of their own culture, and by their motives, intentions and expectations in leaving their own countries. Indians and Pakistanis tend to have a strong sense of their separate nationality and separate culture. In Britain Pakistanis, in particular, often develop a close-knit and independent community life, 'served by their own shops and other services provided by fellow-countrymen'.[17] Rose cites the growth of Pakistani grocers, butchers, cafés, barbers, schools of motoring and banks in areas of Pakistani settlement. And Asians also tend to organise their own housing. The P.E.P. enquiry found that over 70 per cent of both Pakistanis and Indians had never applied to a white landlord for accommodation.[18] The holding aloof from British natives is paralleled by the segregation between different groups of Pakistanis themselves. East and West Pakistanis live apart and West Pakistanis from different regions keep personal relationships to a minimum. Thus the sense of national or regional identity is very strong. Pakistanis in Britain live within their own culture and commonly adopt an 'instrumental' attitude to their life in this country. They come to find work and to earn money and have little desire to adopt or be absorbed into British ways of life, or expectation of this happening. This situation has some short-term advantages. In so far as Asians rely on their own communities for services or social activities, they are less vulnerable to prejudice and rejection. On the other hand, the observance of rules of behaviour very different from those that obtain in Britain creates problems. Asian girls are strictly supervised and thereby handicapped in joining school activities or youth groups. Asian women live secluded and isolated lives, often unable to speak English, often eating separately from the men of the household, but without the compensating support of a wide kin group which would exist in their own country.

The situation of the West Indians is very different. The P.E.P. enquiry suggested that in Britain prejudice against negroes is peculiarly deep-rooted and widespread, and the consequent problems are intensified by the relatively high expectations of West Indians and their lack of any strong sense of independent nationality or culture. 'They came to England as individuals, as kinds of English men, and not as nationals of a state . . . just because they lack a sense of national identity, they do not combine easily . . . .'[19] West Indians come to Britain expecting to be treated as British citizens and depending on British institutions to supply their various needs, and these expectations mean that they are both more exposed to discrimination and also more disappointed by it. 'Many coloured immigrants are protected by their culture and the barrier of language from the full emotional impact of exclusion or rejection . . . but to men and women who see themselves as inheritors of the same culture, the effect of discrimination is far worse.'[20] Even so, the West Indians are not prepared to accept all aspects of British life. As with other groups of immigrants, the discipline exercised over children is usually more strict than is commonly found in British families, so that young West Indians as well as Asians tend to be rather isolated and are less free to mix with British children. Perhaps this strict family control among coloured immigrants is associated with their unusually low delinquency and crime rates.[21]

Far more West Indians than Asians believed that the various services investigated by P.E.P. presented special problems to immigrants[22] and twice as many West Indians as Pakistanis or Indians had experienced discrimination in applying for privately rented houses. There was also a higher proportion of West Indians who experienced discrimination in housing, though the differences in the races here were smaller – 45 per cent of West Indians compared with 35 per cent of Asians.[23]

The disadvantages suffered by coloured immigrants in Britain diminish in certain respects as their residence lengthens. The extent of integration depends on the strength of attachment the immigrant has to a culture which may be very different from the British one, and also on the mutual tolerance of the different groups. Some evidence exists that, while immigrants perform significantly worse than British children on various tests of ability, the gap between the races narrows the longer the time spent in the country.[24] But, in so far as these findings are borne out, the problem of race relations will be intensified. More immigrant children will grow up with qualifications which compare favourably with those of British children, and yet the P.E.P. enquiry showed that it was the ablest and best qualified among the immigrants who suffered most from discrimination. In such circumstances a more highly educated coloured population may well lead to a worsening in race relations. Professional qualifications will enable coloured men to feel they have a just claim to employment on equal terms with white men. Added to this, immigrants will have no other country to which they belong. For those born and bred in Britain, the failure to gain recognition as British citizens is all the more bitter an experience. Rose refers to enquiries in Cardiff and Liverpool which suggest that time does little to bring about easier relations between coloured and white races. 'We see a second and third generation [of coloured immigrants] which lives in a quasi-ghetto, is denied the opportunities available to white English-speaking immigrants, is less ambitious and achieves less than they do.'[25]

Thus economic, social and political position, race and ethnicity all influence the need for and use made of public social services. The rich and the powerful are more independent of public provision, are likely to derive most benefit from it, and also largely control the direction that public policies take. The poor, the uneducated and the inarticulate depend more heavily on public services, tend to use them to less advantage, often receive poorer quality of provision, and are commonly ineffectual as pressure groups for bringing about changes and reforms.

Nevertheless, an admission that social stratification is extremely significant in determining the nature and effectiveness of public welfare policies does not deny the possibility of a move in the other direction. How far do public services, developed within a hierarchical society, reflect and support existing social divisions and how far do they undermine and weaken them?

In trying to determine whether particular social policies are associated with a movement towards greater equality it is important to be clear about the meaning of the term, for it is used in a number of ways. The notion of equality does not imply that people are the same, nor that they should be treated or served in the same way. Provision has to be related to need, and people need different incomes, houses, health or education services according to the number of their dependants, their physical condition and their mental capacities. It is more useful to think of equality as being concerned with equalising 'life-chances' or 'command over resources' which could involve very unequal public provision – more intensive medical care and education for the sick and the dull than for the well and the clever, for instance. In some cases, of course, the capacity to be made healthy or to be educated may be physiologically severely limited so that there is little possibility of equalising command over resources; but lower earning power or even complete dependency need not be associated with subsistence standards of living. There is room for great variation in the position of dependants relative to the rest of the population. Differences in natural ability and skill will not be eliminated, it is the extent of difference in rewards for different kinds of work and different capacities that is at issue.

So to criticise inequality and to desire equality is not, as is sometimes suggested, to cherish the romantic illusion that men are equal in character and intelligence. It is to hold that, while their natural endowments differ profoundly, it is the mark of a civilised society to aim at eliminating such inequalities as have their source, not in individual differences, but in its own organisation, and that individual differences, which are a source of social energy, are more likely to ripen and find expression if social inequalities are, as far as practicable, diminished.[26]

There is, of course, notwithstanding Tawney's powerful phrases, no general agreement about whether greater social equality, as distinct from higher living standards for the very poor, is desirable. Existing economic differences may be defended and rationalised as permitting interesting variety in styles of life, as recognising and reflecting exceptional ability or service to the community, and as preserving incentives to effort and achievement. But, as Lady Wootton has demonstrated, there are no agreed principles which are or have been used to justify or determine the wages for different jobs,[27] let alone to establish the appropriate standards for those who do not work. The position of the latter has barely been discussed since Beveridge's pronouncements in 1942; it has been assumed since then – until very recently – that dependants should draw from the state only the minimum income necessary for subsistence needs.

Nor is it likely that those who would argue for more equality necessarily have the same aims in mind. For some, whom I have described as liberals, equality of opportunity might represent the object in view; others, whom I have called socialists, would be just as concerned with the inequalities which might remain between those who could use opportunities and those who could not. While some, the liberals among them, would advocate equal provision as representing equal opportunities and fair shares for all, others, including the socialists, would urge that equality of opportunity could only be fully realised through unequal treatment for unequal needs to compensate for special disadvantages and in an attempt to secure, as far as possible, equal results.

Views about the desirability of more or less equality must remain, ultimately, a matter of individual moral conviction. But the actual extent of the changes taking place and the effects of government policy are matters capable, at any rate in principle, of objective demonstration.

Since the Second World War there has been a great expansion of government activity in domestic affairs in Britain. Health, education, welfare services and programmes supplying cash benefits of various kinds have all developed along universal lines available to people largely on the basis of need rather than in accordance with ability to pay. The so-called welfare state has emerged. Nevertheless, it is very doubtful whether the various welfare measures have significantly modified the stratification system – at any rate in relation to class and power, though there seems to have been a trend towards more social equality. This is a vitally important matter in so far as it is inequalites rather than standards of living below subsistence which pose the major problems for industrial countries. The question then becomes one of the nature and extent of inequality in Britain. How does it affect and how is it affected by the welfare policies which have been developed, particularly since the Second World War?

The influence of government policies, as distinct from other elements in the stratification system, on the distribution of particular goods and services is examined in later chapters, but first it is appropriate to consider Professor Marshall's thesis on the relation between public social services and equality, a thesis presented while the post-war Labour Government was attempting to establish a welfare state. The analysis of citizenship in terms of civil, political and social rights is well known and it is the discussion of social rights that is of special interest here.[28] Marshall points to a significant movement towards greater social equality which has occurred during this century and which, he argues, has been supported and encouraged by the growth of universal social services such as national insurance, the National Health Service and a national education system. He goes on to enquire into the effects of the increasing equality of status – as the social rights of citizenship have gradually extended to the whole population – on the economic inequalities which he assumes must remain an unavoidable feature of a capitalist economy, and he concludes that growing social equality makes economic inequality less and less significant.

Two questions arise immediately. Is it true that universal social services lead to greater social equality, and what is the relationship between equality of status and economic inequality? Professor Marshall sees universal social services as leading to greater social equality in so far as different economic groups are brought together to share a common experience in contributing to national insurance, drawing family allowances, using the same schools and the same hospitals. The fact that everybody is entitled to similar standards of treatment or service implies an equality of status which is more important than inequality of income: 'Equalisation is not so much between classes as between individuals within a population which is now treated for this purpose as though it were one class.'[29] Not only are the distinctions produced by economic differences undermined as different groups take part in common activities, but they also become less significant as more vital services are provided without reference to individual income but in response to need.

There are a number of problems about Professor Marshall's analysis. One is the question of cause and effect. It is probably true that class divisions in Britain have become less rigid during the twentieth century than they were in the nineteenth, but it would be rash to attribute this to the development of a particular kind of social legislation. It would seem more plausible that the opposite were the case – that is, that a softening of class hatred and prejudice in response to political and economic pressures, a more sophisticated understanding of the situation of the poor and egalitarian ideals, opened the way to policies offering similar standards of treatment and service to the whole population. Perhaps it worked both ways; changing political attitudes allowed the development of universal services which in turn strengthened the already growing feelings of solidarity and equality.

There are other difficulties which are more central to Professor Marshall's argument. How far is it true that universal social services foster a kind of social equality, or equality of status, which is more important than equality of income? In some cases the standard of service offered and the administrative procedures employed seem to nullify any equalising tendencies. It is hard to believe, for instance, that the possession of a national insurance card, signifying participation in a universal scheme, does much to weaken class divisions. More important from this point of view than the national insurance card is the standard of living that the national programme provides. Where, as in Great Britain, the standard is pretty much based on minimum subsistence, the contrast in the situation of those who depend entirely on the state and those who have additional resources of their own is very marked. Class position, in enabling the better-off to run their own welfare systems, seems more effective in strengthening social divisions than membership in a universal scheme in weakening them. The 'general reduction of risk and insecurity' does not necessarily count for very much. More important is the degree of protection offered by the state, and where this is minimal inequalities in personal income remain highly significant and equality of status is less important.

The education service presented Professor Marshall with problems of a rather different kind. Referring to the 1944 Education Act, he remarked that respect for individual rights could hardly be more strongly expressed, and went on to argue that the essence of educational rights is equality of opportunity rather than the provision of similar education for all. For Marshall, selection in education was an acknowledgement of the varying ability of different children. In practice the Education Act has proved ineffectual in bringing about more equal opportunities.[30] Although more children now go on to higher education, the chances of a working-class child compared with those of a middle-class child are as poor as they were forty years ago. This is partly because the universal service that might have been created has not in practice materialised: it is still possible to buy education of higher quality privately, and within the state system, which is used by the great majority, standards of different schools vary significantly. Just as important is the fact that a child's performance in school is greatly influenced by his social background. Middle-class and working-class children of similar ability have substantially different levels of achievement even though they are taught by the same teachers in the same schools. In other words, shared experiences may not be so powerful in bringing about greater equality as Professor Marshall hoped. On the contrary financial poverty, associated as it often is with a particular culture and set of values, may undermine the intention of the universal services to prove similar opportunities for all.

This is in no way to deny the attractiveness of Professor Marshall's conception of citizenship as a basis for the ordering of social relations and the distribution of public services. It is rather to question how far the kind of equality of status that citizenship implies does or can in fact reduce in any substantial way the effects of gross inequalities of income and wealth. Certainly, experience in Britain since the last war suggests that the mere provision of cash grants, health, education and welfare services, theoretically available to everyone on equal terms, by no means guarantees that they will be equally used and therefore that discriminatory policies may be needed to ensure true equality of opportunity.[31] Meanwhile, the character of social stratification in Britain is widely held to have altered in the direction of what may be called 'classless inequality'. In other words, it may be that the citizenship principle has waxed and class feeling waned without any marked change in the degree of inequality in opportunities or living standards.[32]

It is important to be aware of the extent of inequality in income and wealth before going on to examine the distribution of other goods and services. In fact, the distribution of income and wealth within capitalist and free-enterprise societies is largely the outcome of market forces modified in varying degrees by government taxation policies and by social-security schemes and other welfare programmes. The nature of that distribution is of crucial importance in the stratification system and it is worth while, therefore, looking at the extent of the inequalities involved. Economic differences are perhaps easier to measure than differences in status and power, yet the attempt to do so and particularly to assess changes over time is beset with problems.[33]

In the United Kingdom official statistics on the distribution of wealth did not become available until 1971. It was then revealed that in 1969 4 per cent of the population owned 37 per cent, and 9 per cent owned 51 per cent, of all personal wealth, while three-quarters of the population shared between them only one-quarter.[34] The unequal distribution is very striking,[35] though appears to be less marked than for earlier years.[36]

There are a number of ways of approaching the question of income distribution, but enquiries in this country and the United States all point to great inequalities which persist even after tax. R. J. Nicholson has examined the distribution of personal income in the United Kingdom before and after tax for the years 1949–63.[37] He found that during the whole period the position of both the top 1 per cent and the bottom 30 per cent had worsened relatively to the rest; up to 1957 there was a partial trend to greater equality, the share of the top 10 per cent dropping and that of the next 60 per cent rising, though the position of the bottom 30 per cent worsened. Between 1957 and 1963, however, the limited movement towards equality ceased; the top 2 to 40 per cent improved their relative position while the share of the bottom 60 per cent shrank. The distribution of income after tax[38] shows a similar partial trend to greater equality up to 1957 which was then reversed.[39] Thus the share of the bottom 30 per cent in total personal income both before and after tax dropped steadily between 1949 and 1963. A comparison of the situation of different groups before and after tax for particular years shows direct taxation working to the advantage of the bottom 70 per cent and particularly of the bottom 30 per cent. Nevertheless, a distribution which gives 16 per cent of all income to the richest 5 per cent and 12 per cent to the poorest 30 per cent is notably uneven.

Michael Stewart has recently referred to the three ways in which governments may bring about more equality of income – by trying to influence the original distribution that emerges from the play of market forces, by modifying the original distribution by taxation, and by modifying the original distribution through benefits of various kinds – and has analysed developments during the 1960s in these terms.[40] He finds that so far as earnings were concerned, differentials remained much the same : there was no marked improvement in the position of the lowest paid in relation to the rest. On the other hand, the distribution of wealth and pre-tax investment income became slightly more equal during the second half of the 1960s, though for reasons that are rather uncertain and which seem to have little to do with deliberate government policy. Moreover, the tax structure became more progressive in that there was a clear shift towards direct taxes on incomes and away from indirect taxes. Between 1964 and 1970 the yield from indirect taxes rose by 68 per cent but that from direct taxes by 101 per cent. One result of this was that the proportion of income taken in direct taxes for all income ranges, and from single people, married couples and couples with two children, increased between 1964 and 1970 – particularly for the higher income groups. The proportion of disposable income (after direct taxes and benefits) taken in indirect taxes also rose, however, and over all income ranges to a similar degree, so that the government's efforts to concentrate increases on things likely to be bought by the rich rather than by the poor had little effect.

Several attempts have been made to assess the redistributive effects when taxes are considered together with certain welfare benefits, though the type of welfare benefit taken into account differs in different studies. Three enquiries are worth special note. The first[41] examines the redistributive effects of taxes and social-service benefits in the United Kingdom for 1953, 1957 and 1959. It takes account of direct and indirect taxes and social-insurance contributions on the one hand, and cash grants and welfare benefits though school meals, the National Health Service, state education and other subsidies on the other. The study relates to household incomes and is based on Ministry of Labour family-expenditure surveys. The figures demonstrate the very low level at which households began in those years to pay more in taxes than they received in benefits. Of the three types of household analysed it is the household with two adults which gained most between 1953 and 1959 and that of the single adult which fared worst.

A second attempt to determine the break-even level for households in different income ranges in 1964 appears in a United Nations survey[42] which examines changes in the distribution of income for selected countries for which information was available, including the United Kingdom. The United Nations study, like Nicholson's earlier one, takes into account both direct and indirect taxes and national-insurance contributions on the one hand, and cash benefits and benefits in kind on the other. Total taxes paid and benefits received are expressed as a percentage of original household income and this gives clear evidence of the regressive nature of the tax system. The lower-income groups paid the highest proportion of their income in tax. Social-service benefits in cash and kind, in contrast, represented a higher proportion of the income of the poorer groups but the break-even point was very low; households with incomes over £382 were net losers. The study does not distinguish households of different composition.

A later attempt to establish the break-even point for various kinds of family is reported in *Policy for Poverty* and refers to the situation in 1966.[43] This suggests a break-even point of £550 for one adult and £900 for two adults, for two adults and a child and for two adults and two children. This is only a partial measure of the extent to which benefits that are received cancel out taxes that are paid, for it only takes into account direct taxes and ignores indirect taxes and social-security contributions, both of which are regressive and which would, if included in the calculations, lower the break-even point.

Figures quoted by Stewart for the period 1964–9 are more revealing because they aim to reflect how far the final distribution of income, taking into account all taxes and benefits, varies from the original one.[44] Table 3.2 shows the percentage change in income for different income groups and different types of household for selected years and

TABLE 3.2

Per cent change in original income resulting from all taxes and benefits in 1964 and 1969 for selected household types, United Kingdom
(£s per year)

Household	Range of original income			
1 adult	315–82	460–559	676–816	988–1196
1964	−9	−17	−31	−30
1969	+40	+8	−23	−32
2 adults				
1964	+66	−4	−16	−28
1969	+91	+43	+1	−20
2 adults 1 child				
1964			−13	−19
1969			−9	−20
2 adults 2 children				
1964			−5	−12
1969			+19	−4

SOURCE: *The Labour Government's Economic Record 1964–1970*, ed. Wilfred Beckerman (Duckworth, 1972) table 2.22.

indicates a lower break-even point than suggested in *Policy for Poverty*. In so far as comparisons are worth while over this very short period of time, the figures quoted by Stewart also show that the effects of government intervention were more favourable to the lower-income groups in 1969 than in 1964 and less favourable to the higher ones. To this extent there was a slight move towards greater equality of income.

Kolko denies that welfare spending has any equalising effect in the American system. It would theoretically be possible for revenues from regressive taxation to be used to provide welfare services for the poor and so reduce the inequality of incomes. But this he asserts (though without providing any detailed evidence) has not happened: 'welfare spending has not changed the nature of income inequality, nor raised the standard of living of the lowest income classes above what it would have reached if they had not been subjected to federal taxation.'[45] Furthermore, he argues, it is common knowledge that tax avoidance by the rich may conceal the true extent of the inequality of incomes and wealth which presently exist. Both Professor Kolko, and Professor Titmuss (in more detail),[46] point to the various methods employed to reduce tax liability.

Another way of looking at the distribution of incomes is to compare the living standards of those dependent on the state with the average earnings for manual work. A direct way in which governments may improve the position of the worst off (many of the sick, the unemployed and the old who do not pay taxes) is by increasing the various state benefits. Figures which trace the relationship between benefits and average earnings suggest that in the post-war period benefits have remained at a fairly constant proportion of earnings.[47] But if the comparison is made in terms of disposable incomes the picture is rather different. As Stewart shows (see Table 3.3, p. 46) the increase in insurance benefits, between 1963 and 1969 at any rate, was greater than in earnings so that the relative position of pensioners to those in work actually improved.

Various points emerge from this brief survey of the facts of income distribution. First, incomes in the United Kingdom are extremely unequal – the top 10 per cent of all income units received nearly 30 per cent of personal income before tax in 1964; the bottom 10 per cent received 2 per cent. The share of the bottom 20 per cent dropped between 1954 and 1964, but there was also a fall in the income share of the top decile group mainly borne by the top percentile group.[48] The experience of other European countries is outlined in the United Nations survey. Of eight countries examined, only Norway showed a clear trend towards greater equality of income during the late fifties and early sixties, while incomes in France, Sweden and Finland became more

TABLE 3.3

Increases in disposable incomes between 1963 and 1969
(1963 Index = 100), United Kingdom

	Male manual workers	Male administrative, technical and clerical	Retirement pension for married couple
Gross average weekly earnings/income	154	148	149
Disposable income (2-child family)	141 (139)	137 (134)	149
Real disposable income[a] (2-child family)	111 (109)	108 (106)	115

[a] Reduced to allow for rise in appropriate retail-price index
SOURCE: *The Labour Government's Economic Record*, table 2.17.

unequal. In the United Kingdom, the Netherlands, West Germany and Denmark the proportion of income received by the top tenth fell, though the experience of the bottom groups varied.[49] The total effects of tax systems are in general proportional or regressive so that tax policies have not substantially altered the initial distributions. Social-service benefits in cash and kind seem to have modified the pattern a little, but the level of income at which redistribution stops is very low. In the United Kingdom the cash incomes of those supported by the state have barely changed since 1948 in relation to the income of the average manual worker, though a comparison of disposable incomes shows a slight relative improvement for dependants in the late 1960s.

All attempts to measure the effects of government policies are to some degree unsatisfactory and should be treated with great caution. Webb and Sieve point out that Nicholson's studies of the situation in the 1950s leave out of account, among other things, welfare payments such as child allowances, which are made through the tax system, and other tax concessions, such as tax relief to owner-occupiers, which are not allocated as benefits. In this way Nicholson probably overestimates the equalising effects of taxation and benefits on the original distribution of incomes. There are also problems in generalising on a national basis about the net gains or losses of particular income groups as factors other than those considered by Nicholson, for instance whether a wife is earning, may make a substantial difference to the liability to tax.[50] Similarly, very large differences in the subsidies available to council tenants in different local authorities, for example, make calculations based on the notion of national averages misleading, as do regional and local variations in the use of different services.

46

There is a further problem in that certain indivisible benefits, arising for example from public spending on defence or environmental services, are not allocated at all in the studies of redistribution so that conclusions are inevitably partial and distorted.

On the basis of their analysis of the difficulties of trying to measure the extent of redistribution and their judgement about the reliability of the attempts that they examine, Webb and Sieve reach a number of important conclusions. First, 'redistribution studies do not and cannot compare the distribution of post redistribution income in our present society with that which would obtain if the social services did not exist.'[51] They provide some evidence about a much more limited question – the redistributive effects of particular arrangements for providing benefits and raising taxes. 'What they cannot begin to do is estimate the redistribution of initial incomes which occurs when a society establishes social services, modifies a market-based equilibrium and modifies the role, power and rates of growth of various service occupations.'[52] In other words, the comparison of an actual income distribution with one which would exist if taxes and benefits were disregarded is misleading because the original distribution is hypothetical; the very existence of precisely those taxes and benefits which are counted in the calculation of the degree of redistribution which occurs, implies a range of other government measures which would represent a substantial departure from an entirely non-redistributive society.

However, despite reservations about the various attempts to measure income distribution, two general conclusions may still be drawn from the findings of the different studies. Nicholson's enquiries suggest that for given years in the 1950s and combined effects of taxes and benefits did in practice lead to a reduction in inequality of 22 per cent in 1959 and slightly less in 1957. There are clear implications for policy : direct taxes and welfare benefits tend to be progressive while indirect taxes have a regressive effect, so that greater dependence on expenditure taxes and reductions in income tax or on spending on welfare payments will have inegalitarian results.

If changes in redistribution over periods of time are to be considered, the situation seems to be that post-redistribution incomes were as unequal in the post-war as in the pre-war period. In other words, inequalities in final incomes remained constant before, during and after the setting up of the welfare state. Disposable income became slightly more equal between 1937 and 1948, but in later years the trend was reversed and by the end of the 1950s the position was similar to that in 1937 and appears to have remained so throughout the 1960s, with perhaps a marginal improvement for dependants on state benefits towards the end of that period.[53] This is clear evidence of the remarkable power of the existing stratification system through a period, especially

47

in the late 1940s, of considerable pressure towards a more egalitarian society.

Income-maintenance programmes in themselves may be more or less redistributive in transferring cash from rich to poor depending on how they are financed, how benefits are distributed, and the populations that are covered. The more schemes depend on general revenues and the higher proportion of those revenues that are raised by direct and progressive taxes on incomes, the more likely they are to be redistributive. The more benefits are paid in accordance with a means test and are thus restricted to the poor, the more they tend to bring about greater economic equality, though the method of administration may imply or emphasise social inequality.[54] To the extent that benefits are distributed without a test of need, either at a flat rate or proportionate to income, then benefits go to the 'non-poor' as well as to the poor and the redistributive effect is lessened. Similarly, in so far as programmes are restricted to the working class or to the economically poorer classes, they tend to lead to more economic equality; in so far as they are universal in the sense of including the whole population, the more they benefit the relatively rich as well as the poor and the smaller their effect in reducing economic inequalities however desirable they may be on other grounds.[55] It is misleading, however, to speak of any of these factors singly as tending to bring about more or less redistribution; it is the combined effect of methods of financing and paying benefits which is significant.

In Britain the redistributive elements in the income-maintenance programme seem to be getting weaker. The state social-security system is, however, only one part of the total provision against loss of income. As Professor Titmuss has pointed out, fiscal and industrial welfare arrangements also exist which benefit only certain groups in the population but which nevertheless represent a charge on the whole community. Tax allowances for dependants or for occupational welfare schemes are a recognition of needs which involve a loss of revenue for the exchequer which has to be made up from other sources. Moreover, it is the more highly paid workers who tend to benefit most from such concessions.

In such ways existing inequalities may be supported by government policies. Similar trends appear in other services where the relatively rich receive allowances from the state which some estimates suggest are as large or larger than those which go, often in a different form, to the average earners or to the relatively poor. Owner-occupiers as a group are richer than council tenants or those renting dwellings privately, and generally they also live in the most expensive houses. Nevertheless, the allowances they receive through tax relief on mortgage-interest payments have until very recently been similar to the government and local authority subsidies received by council tenants – average earners generally – while the private tenants, the poorest group, have received no public help towards their housing costs.[56] Housing is not, of course, officially regarded in this country as a social service where supply has to be related to an assessment of need. On the contrary, the supply of dwellings is left largely to the market, to be determined by effective demand. It would thus be unlikely that housing policies would exhibit egalitarian features. Only relatively recently have proposals been advanced to alter the various forms of public subsidy available to different tenure groups in such a way as to concentrate help on the poorest and withdraw it from everyone else by making financial grants dependent on a test of need.[57] One of the effects of the recent legislation,[58] however, will be to withdraw existing subsidies from the poorer groups in the population while retaining them for the richer.

With education and health the expressed aims of policy are different. In the 1940s the public authorities became responsible for providing education appropriate for the ages and abilities of all children. Writing shortly afterwards, Marshall remarked that respect for individual rights could hardly be more strongly expressed.[59] He went on, however, to doubt how far it would be realised in face of the demands imposed on the educational system by the economy and the resulting need for a selective process which would inevitably limit rather than extend equality of opportunity. These doubts have proved fully justified, but it is not only selection that has interfered with educational equality of opportunity.[60]

The National Health Service also offers in principle a comprehensive range of services to anyone in need of medical care. Here equality would involve equal provision for treatment of similar needs and equal opportunities for all persons to use medical services, irrespective of economic or social differences. As with schools, however, the supply of health services is very uneven and geographic inequalities are marked. The ratio of doctors and nurses to population varies in different areas and there is some evidence that it is the areas of greatest need that are worst served.[61] There is evidence that some groups, particularly old people, are medically neglected and that they suffer a substantial amount of preventable ill-health. The effects of economic and social differences on the quality of medical care is less certain; few adequate independent measures exist of the incidence of sickness among different social groups so that the exact interpretation of statistics about the use of hospital or G.P. services is hazardous. Even though in some respects the semi-skilled and unskilled appear to be the greatest users of the Health Service, the significance of this fact cannot be assessed without some independent assessment of relative need. There is no doubt, however, that the health standards of the population vary considerably between different regions and different social classes. Such differences probably reflect differences in environmental conditions and in physical constitution as well as differences in medical attention, though, as we have seen, the quality of provision does itself vary and there has been little attempt to explore the possibilities of any sort of compensatory health programme along the lines of the plans for compensatory education. There is little doubt that social stratification in its complex and subtle ramifications of sex and age as well as in its more familiar aspects of income, social position and power is as significant in influencing the distribution of medical services as in education, housing, income or wealth.

In conclusion, inequalities in the primary distribution of income and wealth in Britain are only slightly modified by the taxation system. In welfare policy two main kinds of inequality persist. Even in the universal services standards are often low and vary geographically but there are also differences in the extent to which different social groups or classes benefit from the services that do exist. Social, economic and cultural circumstances all affect the way in which services are used. In particular, the middle classes make more use of education; they keep their children at school longer and send more of them to universities, so that more public money is spent on the education of middle-class than of working-class children.[62] The administrative procedures and traditions attached to particular services are also important in determining how extensively they are used. Poor standards or unpopular conditions of eligibility may deter applications for help, and poor publicity may leave people ignorant of benefits to which they are entitled. In this way services intended to be available for everyone in fact remain unused. Thus economic, social and political stratification are all highly significant in determining the impact of social services as well as in moulding their development.

NOTES

1. *Poverty Amid Plenty.* The Report of the President's Commission on Income Maintenance Programs (U.S. Government Printing Office, 1969).

2. Peter Townsend (ed.), *The Concept of Poverty* (Heinemann, 1970).

3. Wilfred Beckerman, *International Comparisons of Real Income* (O.E.C.D., 1966).

4. That is, statutory schemes of medical care, insurance and family allowances.

5. International Labour Office, *The Cost of Social Security 1964–66* (Geneva, 1972) part 2, comparative tables.

6. United Nations, *Demographic Year Book 1971* (New York, 1972).

7. United Nations, *Demographic Year Book 1972* (New York, 1973).

8. J. E. Meade, *Efficiency, Equality and the Ownership of Property* (Allen & Unwin, 1964) p. 25.

9. There are twelve such projects in different parts of Britain. They were initiated in 1968 as part of the urban programme then introduced by the Prime Minister. The intention is to experiment with ways of improving the quality and effectiveness of local social services in selected areas characterised by poverty and other social problems. Local teams are appointed to develop activities and the action programmes are evaluated in collaboration with university research teams.

10. For discussion of American experience in a variety of community-development experiments, see Peter Marris and Martin Rein, *Dilemmas of Social Reform* (Routledge & Kegan Paul, 1967); Daniel P. Moynihan, *Maximum Feasible Misunderstanding* (Free Press, 1969); and James L. Sundquist (ed.), *On Fighting Poverty* (Basic Books, 1969).

11. It is not only the relations between races that are at issue, even though they may give rise to the most intractable and acute problems. The United States, and many of the rich European countries, recruit workers from the poor parts of Europe for low-paid jobs, and such minority groups may live very uneasily with the native populations – and with each other.

12. Otis Dudley Duncan, 'Inheritance of Poverty or Inheritance of Race?', in *On Understanding Poverty*, ed. Daniel P. Moynihan (Basic Books, 1968) p. 100.

13. Juliet Cheetham, 'Race and Immigration', in *Trends in British Society since 1900*, ed. A. H. Halsey (Macmillan, 1972) table 14.5. The apparently favourable position of the Indian immigrants is explained by their tendency to establish themselves as small-scale entrepreneurs – often shop or restaurant owners.

14. W. W. Daniel, *Racial Discrimination in England* (Penguin, 1968).

15. Ibid. p. 155.

16. Ibid. p. 209.

17. E .J. B. Rose *et al.*, *Colour and Citizenship* (Oxford University Press, 1969) p. 443.

18. Daniel, *Racial Discrimination in England*, p. 41.

19. Rose *et al.*, *Colour and Citizenship*, p. 432.

20. Ibid. p. 438.

21. Ibid. pp. 357, 440, 487.

22. The services in question were hire purchase, motor insurance, hotel accommodation, holiday accommodation, hairdressing and entertainment.

23. Daniel, *Racial Discrimination in England*, p. 65.

24. Rose *et al.*, *Colour and Citizenship*, p. 480.

25. Ibid. p. 489.

26. R. H. Tawney, *Equality* (Allen & Unwin, 1964) p. 57.

27. Barbara Wootton, *The Social Foundations of Wages Policy* (Allen & Unwin, 1962).

28. T. H. Marshall, *Citizenship and Social Class, and Other Essays* (Cambridge University Press, 1950).

29. Ibid. p. 56.

30. See below, Chapter 6.

31. See Chapter 9 for further discussion of the problem of trying to use the idea of citizenship as a basis for social legislation.

32. See W. G. Runciman, *Relative Deprivation and Social Justice* (Routledge & Kegan Paul, 1966) for an analysis of the nature and significance of class, status and equality in Britain since the war.

33. See, for instance, R. M. Titmuss, *Income Distribution and Social Change* (Allen & Unwin, 1962); Adrian L. Webb and Jack E. B. Sieve, *Income Redistribution and the Welfare State* (Bell, 1971).

34. Murray Forsyth, *Property and Property Distribution Policy* (P.E.P., 1971).

35. See A. B. Atkinson, *Unequal Shares* (Allen Lane, The Penguin Press, 1972) for a study of the distribution of wealth in Britain and proposals for making it more equal.

36. Estimates quoted by Meade, *Efficiency, Equality and the Ownership of Property*, for 1911–13, for 1936–8 and for 1960, show 10 per cent of the population owning 92 per cent, 88 per cent and 83 per cent respectively of all personal wealth. It is, of course, inconceivable that inequality was so greatly reduced between 1960 and 1969 and the differences in the figures must to some extent reflect different techniques of measurement. No attempt is made here to calculate comparable statistics.

37. R. J. Nicholson, 'The Distribution of Personal Income', *Lloyd. Bank Review* (January 1967).

38. Direct taxes on income only were considered.

39. Nicholson attributed the check in the move to greater equality to the fact that salaries, professional earnings and incomes from rent and dividends rose faster than wages after 1957.

40. Michael Stewart, 'The Distribution of Income', in *The Labour Government's Economic Record 1964–1970*, ed. Wilfred Beckerman (Duckworth, 1972).

41. J. L. Nicholson, *Redistribution of Income in the United Kingdom* (Bowes & Bowes, 1965).

42. United Nations, *Incomes in Post-War Europe: A Study of Policies, Growth, and Distribution* (Geneva, 1967) chap. 6.

43. Anthony Christopher, George Polyani, Arthur Seldon and Barbara Shenfield, *Policy for Poverty* (Institute of Economic Affairs 1970) p. 29.

44. Stewart, in *The Labour Government's Economic Record*.

45. Gabriel Kolko, *Wealth and Power in America* (Praeger, 1962) p. 390.

46. Titmuss, *Income Distribution and Social Change*.

47. V. N. George, *Social Security – Beveridge and After* (Routledge & Kegan Paul, 1968) p. 24; Frank Field, *One Nation : The Conservatives' Record since June 1970*, C.P.A.G. Poverty Pamphlet 12 (September 1972).

48. United Nations, *Incomes in Post-War Europe*, chap. 6, pp. 14, 15.

49. Ibid. chap. 5, p. 17.

50. Webb and Sieve, *Income Redistribution and the Welfare State*, chap. 6.

51. Ibid. p. 102.

52. Ibid.

53. Ibid. pp. 103–9.

54. See R. M. Titmuss, *Commitment to Welfare* (Allen & Unwin, 1968) part III, for a discussion of the problem of how to concentrate services on those who most need them without at the same time imposing the stigma of social inferiority.

55. See Paukert, in *Role of Social Security in Economic Development*, for a discussion of the various types of social-security schemes and the consequences associated with them.

56. See Chapter 7 below, for further discussion of this situation in the light of recent legislation.

57. See, for example, Adela Adam Nevitt, *Housing, Taxation and Subsidies* (Nelson, 1966) chap. 10.

58. *The Housing Finance Act, 1972* (H.M.S.O., 1972).

59. Marshall, *Citizenship and Social Class*.

60. See Chapter 6 below.

61. See Chapter 5 below. Bleddyn Davies has argued that the standards of a range of welfare services, including education, vary geographically in a way quite unrelated to need. See *Social Needs and Resources in Local Services* (Michael Joseph, 1968).

62. John Vaizey, *The Cost of Education* (Allen & Unwin, 1958).

PART II

British Social Services

The minimal level of insurance and assistance grants guarantees that those who depend on them form one group, who are relatively poor;[2] other groups are those who work for low wages or who are members of large families or of families where one parent is missing. If all the figures are put together it seems that in 1970 there were some four million persons actually dependent on supplementary benefit. There would probably be another three million old people and another one million depending on other kinds of insurance benefit, whose resources were not being supplemented and failed to meet their needs or were barely above the supplementary-benefit scales. In addition there were the families of men in work or other families who were living below supplementary-benefit standard, but were either not eligible for or not claiming assistance, who would add another million to the total living at or near the supplementary-benefit level: approximately nine million people in all.[3] Furthermore, 3,516,000 persons received single payments from the Supplementary Benefits Commission in 1970, an indication of another large group living very near the poverty line.

We have already noted that cash income is only one of the factors – though a very important one – which determine individual opportunities. Education, social class, material and cultural environment, and individual personality all have a part to play. But there is a further sense in which money income may be a very poor guide to living standards and, in so far as it is used as a measure of the differences between groups, may seriously underestimate inequalities. This is because there exists alongside the public welfare services a private welfare system, based on occupation, which serves to raise standards of living in all kinds of ways, through pension schemes, housing or car allowances and other benefits in kind which do not figure in the income statistics.

Little information is available about the importance of fringe benefits in general at different income levels, though Lydall quotes a report relating to the United Kingdom which estimates their value as a proportion of basic salary for managerial staff and shows a steady increase from 11 per cent at a salary of £1050 to 31 per cent at a salary of £7000 or more.[4] Fairly comprehensive statistics about occupational pension schemes, however, come from the government and show how far manual and non-manual workers benefit from private arrangements, the level of benefits provided and the cost involved. In 1971 the total number of employees in the United Kingdom was rather under 23 million; 21 million worked for employers who ran pension schemes but only 11 million persons belonged to such schemes.[5] It is clear from Table 4.1 (p. 59) that the chances of an occupational pension were much worse for women than for men, for manual than for non-manual workers and for those in the private rather than the public sector. In 1971 the total income of the pension funds was £2620 million; there

TABLE 4.1

Employees in organisations with pension schemes and those covered for pensions, 1971, United Kingdom (millions)

	Private sector		Public sector		Total	
Non-manual	All employees	Members of schemes	All employees	Members of schemes	All employees	Members of schemes
Men	4·0	3·0	1·7	1·6	5·7	4·6
Women	2·5	0·9	1·5	0·9	4·0	1·8
Manual						
Men	5·8	2·6	2·2	1·5	8·0	4·1
Women	2·7	0·5	0·4	0·1	3·1	0·6
Total	15·0	7·0	5·8	4·1	20·8	11·1

SOURCE: *Occupational Pension Schemes, 1971* (H.M.S.O., 1972).

were about 65,000 different schemes, mainly in the private sector, and three-quarters of them had less than fifty members.

While the membership of private pension schemes is unevenly distributed between occupational groups and between the sexes, the provision made for those who do receive them is also in some ways unsatisfactory. Only 50 per cent of employees had any chance of retaining full pension rights if they voluntarily left their employment, and benefits from employers' contributions were usually conditional or at the employer's discretion; 17 per cent lost all their rights. In some cases pensions might be augmented either at retirement or after a period of retirement to take into account general pay rises or changes in the cost of living. This has occurred in the public sector since the Pensions Increase Act, 1971, but similar arrangements existed for only about 70 per cent of members of private schemes for whom the increase in pension was generally well below the rise in prices. Manual workers were at a disadvantage compared with other employees with respect to opportunities to transfer their pension rights and to their chances of having their pensions increased after retirement. Widows' pensions were an unconditional benefit for only half the members of occupational schemes, though 40 per cent had the option of giving up part of their own pension in return for a pension payable to a widow after death.

It is possible also to look at occupational pensions in terms of those who presently receive them. Among all retired people nearly half the men, 24 per cent of the women, and 11 per cent of widows had some kind of occupational pension in 1965,[6] the proportion in all cases declining with age. Men who had worked in non-manual jobs were more likely to receive pensions than ex-manual workers, and those who had worked in the public sector were better provided for than those who had worked in the private sector. The average rate of pension was 70 shillings (£3.50), which was thought to underestimate the average for all pensioners. Older people received smaller pensions, but more of them had received some augmentation since their pension was awarded. Even so, less than half older men, though rather more older women, had had some increase. At the end of 1971 it was estimated that nearly two and a half million former employees and half a million widows were drawing occupational pensions. By this date the average amount had increased to £6.45 a week, though the median was £4.05 and 40 per cent of payments were less than £3.[7]

Private schemes, then, tend to concentrate on higher-paid workers and on the younger group of retired people, and they are less common among women. Bearing in mind that the very old, women, and those who have had low earnings throughout their working lives are among those most vulnerable to poverty, it is clear that on the whole the poorest draw least benefit from occupational schemes. This is hardly surprising since private schemes are related to the economic structure, and have grown out of the desire to attract and retain labour in certain occupations rather than to remove poverty among the population as a whole.

It is arguable that the public income-maintenance schemes are not directed to removing poverty either, or that, in so far as they are, they do not do it effectively. This is an inevitable state of affairs in so far as public social-security schemes, like private ones, reflect the economic structure of the country and the assumption that standards of living – over and above minimum subsistence – should depend either on the possession of wealth or the willingness and ability to work. In this sense social rights or citizenship rights are determined more by economic power than by political measures. Marshall points to the nineteenth century in Britain as a period when citizenship rights were divorced from economic dependence on the state, in that pauper status meant the sacrifice of personal liberty, voting rights and respectability.[8] He then points to the twentieth century as a period when this separation of social rights and citizenship rights disappears, with social benefits available without stigma and without infringing citizenship status. But the changes Marshall saw in the 1940s were perhaps more limited than he supposed. The social-security scheme then introduced, which was founded on the Beveridge Report, was more comprehensive than previous arrangements, but although it insisted on rights to a wide range of social benefits those rights hinged on work or wealth, and people who had neither were subject to a separate and discriminatory scheme. Although later developments have altered the social-security scheme in some important respects, on the whole the changes have tended to emphasise the links with and the reflection of economic status.

These links were very evident in Beveridge's proposals in 1942 and in the subsequent legislation. The Beveridge plan[9] envisaged cash benefits at a flat-rate minimum standard in return for contributions which depended on either employment income or private resources. Without contributing there was no right to benefit, but the poor could apply for national assistance – a cash grant dependent on a means test and designed to raise family or individual income to subsistence level.

There are two important aspects of these arrangements : first, the insistence on the minimum as an appropriate level of state support for those who became dependent and, second, the linking of benefit as of right to the power to earn or the possession of capital, and the relegation of those who could not contribute to a secondary scheme which was intended to act to some degree as a deterrent. The idea of the minimum benefit, adequate but no more than adequate for subsistence, was fundamental to Beveridge's plan, which is a classic example of the liberal approach to welfare. It expresses the belief that living standards are properly determined by what individuals can earn or save and that collective provision should be restricted to the essentials for survival; and it reflects the fear that more generous benefits from the state might interfere with personal independence and initiative.

> The state in organising security should not stifle incentive, opportunity, responsibility; in establishing a national minimum, it should leave room and encouragement for voluntary action by each individual to provide more than that minimum for himself and his family . . . . Making provision for . . . higher standards is primarily the function of the individual . . . it is a matter for free choice and voluntary insurance.[10]

The parallel schemes of insurance and assistance also underline the way in which social rights depend on some kind of economic contribution through labour or capital. Those who cannot establish their rights in this way have to rely on a form of state help deliberately designed to be less attractive than the insurance schemes, and this should be guaranteed by the enquiry into personal income and resources and by making national assistance conditional : 'it must be felt to be something less desirable than insurance benefit; otherwise the insured persons get nothing for their contributions. Assistance therefore will be given always subject to proof of needs and examination of means; it will be subject also to any conditions as to behaviour which may seem likely to hasten restoration of earning capacity.'[11]

Although the National Insurance and National Assistance Acts adopted many of the essential elements in Beveridge's proposals, the implementation of the programme departed from the original plan in one crucial respect: insurance benefits were not and never have been set at a level high enough to reach the minimum standard which Beveridge recommended. In the event, even people who are fully insured are obliged to apply for assistance if they are to reach the officially defined minimum. The right to a minimum cash income from the state has thus never in practice been observed. A minimum standard of living is not a 'right of citizenship' but is dependent on a man's own resources or on a type of state aid which to a greater or lesser degree humiliates those who receive it. To this extent the social-security system is firmly rooted in *laissez-faire* principles.

The fact that people drawing insurance benefit have had to turn to national assistance has made the deterrent elements in the latter hard to justify, and there have in fact been attempts to soften the system in various ways to make it more acceptable. Nevertheless, there is still plenty of evidence that assistance, however it may be intended, is not regarded or understood as a right – and a substantial number of people who are eligible for it do not in fact apply.

The failure to observe the adequacy principle meant that Beveridge's attempt to set up a system of social rights independent of economic power, even for those included in the insurance scheme, was seriously undermined, and since the 1940s the programme has been further modified in such ways as to make it even more dependent on the market system. This has come about with the gradual abandonment of a second of Beveridge's crucial principles – that of the flat-rate benefit. The linking of benefits to previous earnings – as now happens for the first six months of unemployment and sickness benefit, and to a much smaller degree for pensions – emphasises again the extent to which the power to earn determines the entitlement to benefit even within the public welfare system. But it is more consistent with the liberal than the *laissez-faire* approach to social policy, for it raises the minimum and relates it to prevailing living standards. Successive governments have been slow to introduce wage-related benefits into their pension arrangements, no doubt because pensions represent the most costly element in the insurance scheme, but in 1961 a graduated plan came into effect which provided for slightly higher pensions in return for higher contributions over a given range of earnings. The extra benefits, however, were extremely small. The maximum graduated pension amounted to only £3.50 a year for each year of contributions and the lowest earners received only 38p a year for each year they contributed.[12] Nor were the additional allowances protected against inflation.

In 1969 the Labour Government produced a much more comprehensive plan.[13] It aimed at roughly half-pay on retirement for the average earner in manual work. Those earning more than the average received pensions which were rather less than half-pay up to a ceiling set at one and a half times average earnings after which they remained at a flat rate, and low-paid workers received rather more than half their normal earnings. Thus, while the proposals brought pensions and earnings into a closer relationship, there was to be some internal redistribution, the scheme being slanted to give proportionately lower pensions to the high paid and proportionately higher pensions to the low paid. There was also a gesture towards the idea of the collective responsibility of the working population for the support of the old and a corresponding movement away from the notion that benefits should be determined by individual contributions. Thus it was to be the duty of the minister to adjust pensions in payment every two years to take into account changes in the value of money; pensions could also be raised to take into account changes in general living standards, though any such increases were to be at the discretion of the minister. This is very different to the French arrangements, whereby pensions in payment rise automatically as wages rise, where the principle of individual saving for individual benefit is largely discounted, and where pension schemes are widely accepted as a device for transferring income from those who are working to those who have retired.[14]

One object of the Labour party plan was to relate benefits and contributions to earnings, another was to restore Beveridge's lost principle of adequacy: 'Benefits must normally be sufficient to live on without other means.'[15] This was a move to ensure rights to benefits, at least for those who had paid contributions, but its success would depend on how far the minister chose to use his discretionary power to keep pensions in line with rising living standards. Atkinson has estimated that if pensions were to be increased at the same rate as increases in average earnings, then, under the proposals set out in the White Paper, pensions would be adequate for all except roughly 1 per cent of retired people. The need for supplementary benefit would thus be almost eliminated, though it would still be required for those with very high rents or other special needs. If, on the other hand, pensions were increased only to maintain their real value while assistance levels were raised to keep in line with rising living standards, pensions would be in danger of falling below the official minimum. Atkinson reckons that in these circumstances nearly a third of pensioners would receive pensions below the supplementary-benefits standard – even when the scheme was in full operation.[16] Thus the Labour party proposals would not necessarily have removed more people from supplementary benefit. They would have raised pensions above the minimum as currently defined only in so far as the government of the day chose to adopt the more generous policy.

The Labour administration did not stay in power long enough to turn its proposals into legislation and the Conservatives introduced a rather different plan. Like the Labour proposals it relates benefits to individual income and aims to 'secure . . . that everyone has the opportunity of saving for a pension related to his earnings . . . '.[17] But there is a vital difference in the place accorded by the Conservatives to private schemes. The pension plan contains three elements: the state 'basic' pension at a flat rate financed by earnings-related contributions and exchequer supplement; occupational pensions to provide the earnings-related part of the pension for those who belong to them; and the state 'reserve' scheme to provide a wage-related element for those not covered by an occupational scheme. The state reserve scheme will be financed by contributions alone and there will be no exchequer supplement.

The proposals commit the government to maintaining the real value of the basic pensions by uprating every two years, but increasing the real value remains a matter of discretion. Private schemes also have to protect the value of their pensions after award, but there are no similar guarantees written into the state reserve scheme. This set of proposals underlines yet more strongly the willingness to let market forces determine levels of security. Private occupational schemes are encouraged for those who are in a position to join them and an inferior state reserve scheme will cover those who are not.

So much for the security available in retirement. Provision for men who are working also reflects the values and supposed needs of the economic system more than a conception of social or citizenship rights which are independent of it. Thus until very recently men in full-time employment were not eligible for assistance even though their income might be insufficient for family needs in terms of the official minimum scales. Beveridge recognised this problem and attempted to meet it by advocating a system of family allowances, but the exclusion of the first child and the low rates of allowance have meant that poverty still exists among the families of men who are working.

The introduction of the Family Income Supplement has gone some way to meeting the problem in that it is a scheme for raising family income where the head of the family is employed. A minimum income is set for a one-child family, which is increased for subsequent children. For families falling below that level the F.I.S. amounts to half the deficit, subject to a maximum. Nevertheless, the F.I.S. does not raise the low-paid worker and his family out of poverty. One- and two-children families who paid even moderate rents were still below the supplementary-benefit level in 1971 even after receiving the F.I.S.[18]

A second problem about the Family Income Supplement is that it depends on a means test and on personal application. It is now common knowledge that the public response to such benefits is likely to be poor and, in spite of government publicity efforts, which aimed to secure a 'take up' rate of 85 per cent, only 93,000 awards had been made by December 1971, nearly six months after the scheme came into operation, in relation to 188,000 families whom it had been estimated would be eligible. More recent estimates suggest little change in the proportion of eligible families who claim the benefit.

Apart from the failure of social-security benefits to raise the families of men in work out of poverty, in some cases the welfare system also fails to support those who would appear to be its own special responsibility – those who have no employment income – even at the officially defined minimum. The wage stop is a device for preventing a man out of work from receiving supplementary benefit which exceeds the amount he might expect to earn in employment, even though this would result in an allowance below the Commission's own scales. Between December 1965 and November 1970 the number of unemployed men receiving supplementary benefit rose from 99,000 to 216,000, and the number whose benefit was reduced in accordance with the wage stop increased from 16,000 to 32,000, the average deduction being nearly £2.00.[19] However, Family Income Supplement is available for families claiming supplementary benefit and it will probably reduce the number of dependants on the Commission whose incomes fall below the standard scales.

The character of the public social-security arrangements is in itself significant, but it is equally important to examine the relation between the social-security scheme and other aspects of government policy which bear directly on personal incomes and standards of living. In 1955 Professor Titmuss pointed to the importance of the occupational and fiscal systems, as well as the public social services in distributing welfare benefits.[20] That benefits may be linked to occupation or available through the remission of tax produces serious anomalies and also an overall result which tends to relate larger benefits to larger incomes, which reflects and reinforces existing disparities of income and wealth rather than modifying them. These trends have become more apparent since the publication of Titmuss's lecture. Occupational and private-welfare schemes are spreading, and the relation between the taxation and social-security systems has become extremely complex. As the tax threshold as a proportion of average earnings has dropped and the value of money fallen, the income-tax and social-security systems have come to overlap to such an extent that it is now possible for people whose incomes are below supplementary-benefit level to pay income tax. Similarly, the Family Income Supplement is above the tax threshold for some families, so that a family may pay out in tax what it receives in income supplement. This, as Professor Atkinson remarks, can scarcely reflect deliberate government policy.[21]

There are two possible objectives of income-maintenance programmes.

They may be designed to provide a minimum income, based on the cost of a range of goods conventionally defined as necessities, in times when income ceases for some reason or in recognition of the various kinds of dependency. Alternatively, programmes may be designed not to provide a minimum, but to compensate for loss of earnings or to help to meet the costs of dependency at a level which is related to the recipient's normal income. The former objective would require flat-rate benefits based on the cost of certain essentials; the latter implies variable benefits which would reflect to some degree the different living standards and capacities to earn of those who received them. The former is consistent with the *laissez-faire* conception of welfare outlined above. The latter fits better into the liberal model.

In Britain the public state welfare system has until recently pursued the first objective, while the welfare benefits linked to occupation or available through the fiscal system have tended to follow the second. The combined effects of the various methods of distributing assistance have resulted in a complex situation where estimates of the total benefits from the various sources for families in different income groups and of different composition are extremely hazardous. Nevertheless, if we take one of the more obvious features of the British arrangements, it is clear that even the first possible objective of an income-maintenance scheme, that of providing a minimum income for all persons, is not at present realised.

This situation has produced a number of proposals for reform – some of which have found their way into government programmes. There are plans to increase the value of insurance benefits, pressure to increase family allowances and to concentrate them on the poor, attempts to persuade the government to legislate for a minimum wage, and the introduction of the Family Income Supplement as an alternative device for helping families where the head of the family is in full-time employment.

All these proposals represent attempts to deal with poverty among particular groups – pensioners, families with children, low-paid workers – and are a continuation of the unco-ordinated approach which has been characteristic of British policies to deal with financial poverty. The lack of co-ordination is evident in the large number of services and benefits available on various means tests. Different standards of need are employed by different grant-giving bodies, and failures in publicity, popular resistance to enquiries into means, and misunderstanding of eligibility conditions all result in many benefits remaining unclaimed. The failure to relate policies to one another can also lead to the so-called 'poverty-trap' – a situation where increased earnings for low-paid workers may be largely cancelled by extra payments which have to be made for different means-tested benefits as income rises. In some cases additional earnings may mean that net income falls as the increased tax paid – either explicitly through liability to income tax or implicitly through loss of means-tested benefits, or both – may amount to over 100 per cent.[22]

This underlines the problem not only of the incoherent nature of the welfare system itself but also of the complete failure to relate welfare and tax policies. We have reached a situation where, on the one hand, people whose incomes are below the official minimum may yet be liable to direct taxation, and where, on the other hand, more substantial benefits may be available to higher-income groups through remission of tax than to low earners through direct welfare payments. Whether this represents a problem, of course, depends on assumptions about the purpose of social policy; about how far the different allowances should reflect existing patterns of income distribution or how far they sholud serve to modify them.

A more comprehensive approach to the reform of social-security arrangements would be one which considered the welfare and tax systems together, so that the two sets of arrangements would be mutually consistent and designed to bring about whatever degree of redistribution was thought desirable. One strategy would be to raise the tax threshold so that liability to direct taxation could not occur until well above both the supplementary-benefit level and the level of eligibility for other means-tested services. This would imply separating the tax and welfare systems to prevent the former cancelling out or reducing the latter. A second strategy could involve an amalgamation of the two systems through some form of negative taxation plan.[23] Under such an arrangement benefits, or negative taxes, would be paid by the tax authorities to individuals or families whose income was below a given level and tax would be paid to the tax authorities by individuals or families whose income was above the given level. There are many possible variants of such a plan.[24] Particular proposals differ as to the level of income to be guaranteed, whether this should be below or correspond to the poverty line, and in the tax rate to be levied on earnings and thus the extent to which benefits would be payable to those whose incomes were above the minimum. The lower the tax rate, the higher the income level at which benefits would be cancelled out by taxes and the more expensive the scheme. The higher the tax rate, the more the scheme would be confined to those living below the minimum but the greater would be the interference with financial incentives to work.[25]

Under a negative taxation scheme benefits could replace grants, now paid through the welfare system, and allowances, which could be set against taxation. Alternatively, a negative tax plan might be supplementary to existing arrangements for welfare and fiscal benefits. The recent proposal for a tax-credit scheme in Britain is a compromise in that it suggests replacing some but not all of the benefits at present received under the welfare and tax systems. It would introduce tax credits to take the place of the main income-tax personal allowances and the family allowances which form part of the social-security arrangements.[26] Credits would be paid to all persons eligible, with additions for dependants. Where credits exceeded tax due, then the difference would be received as an addition to income; where tax liability exceeded credits the difference would be deducted in taxation.

The gains to the poor of any such scheme depend, of course, on how comprehensive it is, on the value of the credits, and on the rate of taxation. The scheme suggested by the Conservatives in 1972 would cover about 90 per cent of the population, excluding the self-employed, very low earners and those neither working nor qualifying for insurance benefits. If introduced at the level recommended in the Green Paper[27] the scheme would reduce the number of pensioners drawing supplementary benefit by over a third, would abolish the need for Family Income Supplement among members of the new scheme, and would increase the income of the low paid, particularly those with dependants. However, some of the poorest in the country would be excluded from the programme and receive no benefit of any kind. The proposals are a step towards rationalising and simplifying the arrangements for supplementing low incomes and supporting children and they do something to concentrate financial help where it is most needed, but they fall far short of a comprehensive and effective plan for abolishing financial poverty.[28]

NOTES

1. Central Statistical Office, *Social Trends*, no. 3 (1972) table 31.

2. In 1973 the flat rate for the insurance pension was £7.75 and for unemployment and sickness benefit £7.35 a week for a single person with an additional earnings-related supplement during the first six months. At the same time, the supplementary-benefit scales allowed £7.15 plus rent, and in 1972 the average rent for council tenants, the largest tenure group among the Supplementary Benefits Commission's dependants who were householders, was £3.30. There was also in 1973 an addition of £1 a week for long-term cases, so that the total income of a single retired pensioner on supplementary benefit would be approximately £12 a week – a sum representing roughly a third of the average industrial earnings of manual workers.

3. See Appendix A for an explanation of the way in which this figure is reached. For alternative estimates of numbers in poverty see A. B. Atkinson, *Poverty in Britain and the Reform of Social Security* (Cambridge, 1969). Atkinson attempts to count only those living below supplementary-benefit level. See also Brian Abel-Smith and Peter

Townsend, *The Poor and the Poorest* (Bell, 1965). The figures in this study relate to 1954 and 1960 and poverty is defined as an income less than 140 per cent of the current, basic national-assistance scale.

4. Harold Lydall, *The Structure of Earnings* (Oxford University Press, 1968) p. 269.

5. *Occupational Pension Schemes, 1971*, Fourth Survey by the Government Actuary (H.M.S.O., 1972).

6. Ministry of Pensions and National Insurance, *Financial and Other Circumstances of Retirement Pensioners* (H.M.S.O., 1966) appendix V. Memorandum of the Government Actuary's Department.

7. *Occupational Pension Schemes, 1971*. The weekly figures quoted relate to 1970 and are based on the Family Expenditure Survey.

8. Marshall, *Citizenship and Social Class*.

9. Sir William Beveridge, *Social Insurance and Allied Services*, Cmd. 6404 (H.M.S.O., 1942).

10. Ibid. paras 9 and 302.

11. Ibid. para. 369.

12. See G. D. Gilling Smith, *The Complete Guide to Pensions and Superannuation* (Pelican Original, 1967).

13. Department of Health and Social Security, *National Superannuation and Social Insurance*, Cmnd. 3883 (H.M.S.O., 1969).

14. See Tony Lynes, *French Pensions* (Bell, 1967) especially chap. 7.

15. D.H.S.S., *National Superannuations*, Cmnd. 3883, p. 12.

16. Atkinson, *Poverty in Britain*, pp. 114–15.

17. D.H.S.S., *Strategy for Pensions*, Cmnd. 4755 (H.M.S.O., 1971) p. 2.

18 David Barker, 'The Family Income Supplement', *New Society* (5 August 1971).

19. *Department of Health and Social Security Annual Report 1970*, Cmnd. 4714 (H.M.S.O., 1971) table 128; C.P.A.G., *Poverty*, no. 20–1 (Winter 1971).

20. R. M. Titmuss, 'The Social Division of Welfare', *Essays on the Welfare State* (Allen & Unwin, 1958).

21. A. B. Atkinson, 'Income Maintenance and Income Taxation', *Journal of Social Policy*, vol. 1, part 2 (April 1972). Atkinson also points to the result of the combination of family allowances, Family Income Supplement and tax child allowances, which is far too arbitrary to reflect considered judgements about need.

22. Ibid.

23. These two strategies are distinguished by Professor Atkinson in the article quoted in note 21 above.

24. See Christopher Green, *Negative Taxes and the Poverty Problem* (Brookings Institution, 1967), and J. E. Meade, 'Poverty in the Welfare State', *Oxford Economic Papers*, vol. 24, no. 3 (November 1972).

25. Many proposals have been made for some form of income guarantee. See, for instance, *Poverty Amid Plenty*, The Report of the President's Commission on Income Maintenance Programs; Christopher

et al. Policy for Poverty; C. V. Brown and D. A. Dawson, *Personal Taxation, Incentives and Tax Reform* (P.E.P., 1969). For a detailed study of recent American experience and reactions see Daniel P. Moynihan, *A Guaranteed Income* (Random House, 1972).

26. *Proposals for a Tax Credit System*, Cmnd. 5516 (H.M.S.O., 1972).

27. Ibid.

28. For a criticism of the government's tax-credit proposals see Michael H. Cooper, 'Tax Credits: Problems and Proposals', *Social and Economic Administration*, vol. 7, no. 2 (May 1973).

extent the skill, knowledge and interest of doctors identifies the need and determines the demand for medical care, and if that skill or knowledge or interest is deficient then demand will be correspondingly reduced. This is not to deny that the incidence of sickness also affects demand, as do people's expectations about the standards of health to which they feel themselves entitled, which in turn reflect the level of popular knowledge and understanding of medical techniques. Finally, demand is also influenced by the quality and extent of the services available. It is a difficult business, therefore, to distinguish the need for medical care, given the various circumstances which may serve either to repress or translate it into effective demand : circumstances such as the competence of doctors, the availability of hospital beds, the beliefs and expectations people hold about possibilities of treatment, and whether or not they have the money or other resources to obtain it.

The measures of health that exist are inadequate and unreliable. The most reliable statistics are the mortality figures, which analyse death by cause, age, sex and sometimes by social class; but they reveal relatively little about the state of health of those who are alive. Comprehensive information about the incidence and prevalence of sickness is difficult to find. We have to rely first on statistics about the use of health services – collected sometimes through surveys of samples of the population, sometimes by the various branches of the health service – and second on judgements which people make about their own health.[1] Neither type of data is entirely satisfactory. Consultation rates, hospital statistics and statements about the use of different facilities may be an accurate measure of the use of services, but they are a very uncertain guide to the health of the population; they refer only to the illnesses patients report or for which they seek treatment. In so far as figures are based on people's own assessments of their medical state, they may indicate different conceptions and expectations about health or failures in accuracy or knowledge or memory.[2] Comparisons between classes or regions are particularly hazardous as they may reflect the different habits of different social or geographical groups, or variations in the availability of services, as well as differences in the actual occurrence of sickness.

In considering the facts of distribution as revealed by the statistics, comparisons are made of standards of health and the use and supply of services, between different social classes, geographical areas and kinds of disability. Social class is, of course, a very crude method of distinguishing people. A comprehensive study of the varying standards of health and the varying chances of medical care among the population would call for an examination of the significance of many other differences – as between men and women, the married and the single, and the old and the young, for example – but unfortunately the information we have is too scanty to permit such an analysis.

If we turn from the distribution of health to the distribution of medical services, we find that hospitals and medical personnel are very unevenly spread geographically, as they are between different social classes and different branches of medicine. The significance of this fact is obscured because without reliable measures of the incidence of sickness, we cannot assess the adequacy of the supply, either in terms of the total provision of services or in terms of their distribution. There are also difficulties, of course, in finding ways of assessing the quality and effectiveness of the various health services.[3] Nevertheless, although exact measurements may not be possible, there is enough evidence that British arrangements fail not only to relate medical care to need but also to effective demand.

Having duly noted the problems the data available can now be examined. If we look first at the population's health we find a marked variation in death rates between the social classes. Table 5.1 shows the

TABLE 5.1

Standardised mortality ratios for men[a] and women[b], 1930-2, 1949-53, and 1959-63 by social class, England and Wales

			Class I	Class II	Class III	Class IV	Class V
1930-2	men		90	94	97	102	111
	women	married	81	89	99	103	113
		single	100	64	95	102	112
1949-53	men	published	98	86	101	94	118
		adjusted	86	92	101	104	118
	women	married	96	88	101	104	110
		single	82	73	89	89	92
1959-63	men		76	81	100	103	143
	women	married	77	83	103	105	141
		single	83	88	90	108	121

[a] Aged 15 to 64.
[b] Aged 20 to 64.

SOURCES: Registrar-General, *Decennial Supplement, England and Wales, 1961, Occupational Mortality Tables* (H.M.S.O., 1971); Halsey (ed.), *Trends in British Society*, table 11.7.

standardised mortality ratio[4] for men and women for various periods and it is clear that the differences between the classes, which are obvious enough, have actually increased over the past forty years.[5] Class I, though slightly more likely to die of heart disease than classes II and IV, has a lower death rate than the other classes for practically all the listed illnesses (see Table 5.2, p. 74). Class V has by far

TABLE 5.2

*Standardised mortality ratio for men by social class and cause of death,
1959–63, England and Wales*

	Class I	Class II	Class III	Class IV	Class V
T.B.	40	54	96	108	185
Coronary disease, angina	98	95	106	96	112
Bronchitis	28	50	97	116	194
Malignant neo-plasm	73	80	104	102	139
All causes	76	81	100	103	143

SOURCE: Registrar-General, *Decennial Supplement, England and Wales
1961, Occupational Mortality Tables.*

the heaviest mortality for all the specified diseases, and the death rate
from bronchitis is especially high compared with the other classes.

Infant-mortality rates are often used as a general indicator of the
health of populations and as a reflection of the medical services they
receive, and here the association with class is also marked. In 1964-5
the infant-mortality rate for classes I and II was 12.7 and for classes
IV and V, 20.8.[6] Figures for classes I and V are not distinguished, but
it is fair to assume that they would show even greater variations. Moreover, class differences seem to be widening. Between 1949 and 1964
the fall in still births and neo-natal deaths (deaths of children up to
four weeks) was proportionately greater for social classes I and II.[7]
Class is also significant in maternal mortality. The standardised mortality
ratio for married women between 1962 and 1965 varied from 55 for
class I to 90 for class III and 178 for class V.[8]

Variations in mortality are associated with region as well as with
social class, though the two to some extent overlap. Table 5.3 (p. 75)
shows the disadvantages of living in the North and the North-West and
the advantages of living in the South and East. The still-birth and infant-mortality rates are lower in the South, South-East and South-West
than in any other part of England and Wales; they are highest in Wales
and in the North, particulary the North-West. The urban areas have the
highest rates, and in the large industrial cities such as Liverpool and
Manchester the problem is greatest, in terms of the numbers of deaths.[9]
In 1957 the infant-mortality rate varied between 12 in Wimbledon and
43 in West Hartlepool. The death rate for bronchitis showed even more
dramatic differences, rising from 23 in Esher and 35 in Epsom and
Ewell to 221 in Oldham and 227 in Salford.[10] Differences of this
magnitude no doubt reflect variations in climate, physical environment,
occupation and class; but, whatever their explanation, they demonstrate
the ineffectiveness of the health services in equalising health conditions
in different parts of the country.

TABLE 5.3

Male standardised mortality ratio by region and class, 1959–63, England and Wales

Region	All classes	Class I	Class II	Class III	Class IV	Class V
England and Wales	100	76	81	100	103	143
Northern	111	82	87	113	105	164
East and West Riding	106	73	88	105	109	150
North-Western	116	84	96	114	116	165
North-Midland	94	74	77	92	94	133
Midland	104	73	84	103	106	155
Eastern	84	69	69	84	85	118
London, South-Eastern	94	77	78	94	100	127
Southern	92	70	75	89	92	127
South-Western	93	73	74	92	97	131
Wales	111	78	87	121	110	146

SOURCE: Registrar-General, *Decennial Supplement, England and Wales 1961, Occupational Mortality Tables.*

The General Household Survey is a useful source of information both on chronic and acute illness, based on people's own assessments of their state of health, and on consultations with doctors and the use of other services. There is an inverse relationship between the reporting of chronic sickness and social class, the rate for unskilled manual workers being more than three times that for professional men.[11] Considering thirteen different causes of disability, the semi-skilled and unskilled were more vulnerable in all cases except one, particularly in the case of arthritis and rheumatism, bronchitis and mental disorder.[12] There is also an inverse relationship between chronic sickness and the income of the household head and between chronic sickness and household amenities.[13]

The significance of social class is also apparent in the reporting of absence from work due to sickness. Unskilled men have the highest absence rate and professional workers the lowest. The unskilled lost nearly five times more days a year through illness or injury than the professionals.[14] Not surprisingly, men who describe themselves as dissatisfied with their jobs have more absence through illness than other employed men, a tendency even more marked among women. Thus the unenjoyable nature of their work may partly explain the higher absence rates of the unskilled.

Geographical situation as well as class affects sickness. Variations in the reporting of long-term illness were marked, moving at the extremes from a rate of 127 to 193 per thousand in the outer metropolitan area and Wales respectively.[15] The rate among the widowed, divorced and separated was higher than among married or single people for both sexes and at all ages, though particularly for younger men and women. The rate for acute illness showed similar marked regional variations and, as for chronic sickness, particularly high rates were found in Wales and relatively low rates in East Anglia. As with chronic sickness, married people appeared less affected than others.

Class and region also influence the use of services. If consultations with G.P.s are analysed by social class, class III had the highest consultation rate during 1955-6, followed by IV and V and then II and I,[16] but unfortunately we do not know how far the incidence of sickness between the social classes varied with the different consulting habits. Standardised consulting rates[17] for particular illnesses during the same year showed the highest rates for class V for cancer and, most markedly, for bronchitis, and this corresponded with the highest mortality ratios in each case.[18] Class I showed the lowest consulting rate for each of the listed diseases (including heart diseases for which it had the highest death rate).

The General Household Suvey contains further analysis of consulting rates by socio-economic group. The pattern for 1971 shows the semi-skilled and unskilled workers with the highest overall G.P. consulting rates, though there are considerable variations between different age groups.[19] In particular, it is notable that children under five in the professional and managerial group see a G.P. far more often than children of the same age in the semi- and unskilled manual-worker class. It is extremely unlikely that the differences can be explained by the better health of the latter. Greater anxiety, and perhaps knowledge, about children's health and greater readiness to approach doctors on the part of professional parents seem much more plausible explanations.

Regional differences in consultation rates are also apparent from *The General Household Survey*, with most frequent visits to G.P.s in the North and North-West and Scotland and least in the South-East, West Midlands and East Anglia.[20] Figures for out-patient attendances at hospitals show relatively low rates in the East Midlands and high rates in the Greater London Council area. That is, they seem to bear little relation to the G.P. consulting rates. There is no analysis of out-patient visits by social class.

In spite of the uncertainties of notification rates it is worth while looking at regional differences, as in some cases these seem too great to be explained away in terms of differences in administrative efficiency, though the extent of differences in health that they represent is not clear. Notification rates for T.B. in 1957, for instance, varied from 180 in South Shields to 19 in Dewsbury.[21]

We may now turn from the health of the population to the medical care available. The character of the supply of health services is to some degree bureaucratically controlled, but it is also influenced by what people will pay and, in any case, is substantially determined by professional interests. A consideration of the distribution of medical care shows marked variation in different parts of the country, between different classes, and between different kinds of disability and sickness.

There are a number of indices that can be used to measure differences in supply. If we first consider the situation of teaching and non-teaching hospitals we find that of several hundred hospitals classified as 'acute' there are only 30 teaching hospitals and that 16 of these are in London. The average cost per week for in-patients in acute hospitals in 1973 varied from £129 in the London teaching hospitals to £116 in the provincial teaching hospitals to £92 in non-teaching hospitals;[22] and while there are nearly three times as many consultants working in the non-teaching as in the teaching hospitals, only a quarter of them hold merit awards, compared with more than half of those in teaching hospitals.[23] The geographical concentration of the teaching hospitals is apparent in that while 15 per cent of all patients in England and Wales admitted to acute hospitals entered teaching hospitals in 1966, the proportion was under 7 per cent in Sheffield and Manchester compared with 28 per cent in the Metropolitan and Oxford regions.[24]

The ratio of consultants to population may also be considered as an indication of the quality of medical care, and in 1970 this varied from 20 for every 100,000 persons in the Metropolitan areas to 12 for every 100,000 in Sheffield.[25] Furthermore consultants holding merit awards are concentrated in the South. 35 per cent of all consultants in England and Wales hold merit awards, but 40 per cent of those in the Metropolitan regions hold them in contrast with 30 per cent in Leeds, Birmingham, Manchester and Sheffield.[26] The ratio of hospital beds to population shows similar variations, with the extremes in 1969 of seven for every 1000 persons in Sheffield and 13 per 1000 in the South-West Metropolitan area.[27]

Such figures are, however, a very incomplete guide to the total supply of medical services in different areas; their significance could be quite altered by a different distribution of G.P.s and other domiciliary services. In practice the pattern is not modified in this way. In 1963 Sheffield also had the smallest proportion of G.P.s and the Metropolitan areas the highest, 27 and 53 per 1000 population respectively.

The central department has made more positive efforts to equalise the geographical distribution of G.P.s than that of hospital doctors,[28] and it was particularly successful in the 1950s and up to 1961 during a period when increasing numbers of doctors were entering general practice. Between 1952 and 1961 the proportion of patients living in 'underdoctored' areas dropped from 52 to 17 per cent. After 1961, however, the position worsened as the number of doctors in general practice declined. By 1967 the proportion of patients in underdoctored areas had risen to 34 per cent of the population, and the average number of patients for each doctor in such districts was 2840, compared with 1837 in the most-favoured areas, which contained 8 per cent of the population.[29]

The geographical distribution of dentists in relation to population is also notably uneven. They are concentrated in the South and South-East and are rarest in the Midlands, the North, East Anglia and Wales. County boroughs tend to be better served than counties, and this pattern for Health Service dentists is reinforced by the distribution of dentists in private practice.[30] One measure of dental care is supplied by the average payment per person. In 1967–8 this varied from half the national average of £1 9s 4d in Brecon and Norfolk to more than double that figure in Chester.[31] If the proportion of the population seen as patients, including both the general public and schoolchildren, is examined, the average for England and Wales turned out to be 22 per cent, but while the Metropolitan areas all had above average proportions, with 38 per cent in the South-West Metropolitan region, Leeds, Birmingham and Sheffield dropped to 16 per cent or less.

There are further marked variations in the domiciliary health services provided by local authorities. The local health-authority areas have not in the past corresponded to the hospital regions and it would be difficult to work out precisely how far shortages in one branch of the service are compensated by generous provision in another. But a glance at the situation for some of the authorities in the Sheffield area does not suggest that the local-government services are particularly strong. In 1965 local authorities in the Sheffield hospital region employed on average 0.10 health visitors, 0.18 home nurses and 0.13 midwives for every 1000 of the population, compared with an average for the country of 0.12, 0.18 and 0.12.[32] Nor does the level of provision reflect a low level of need. Moser and Scott's comparative study of 157 British towns shows Sheffield with an average infant-mortality rate, but a relatively low expectation of life, relatively high death rates from cancer and bronchitis and a high notification rate for T.B.

As we have seen, the problems involved in measuring standards of service on the one hand, and needs on the other, and of relating the two, are formidable,[33] but the available evidence suggests that so far as geographical distribution is concerned there is little or no correlation between the provision of and need for services. If we look at the distribution of services from another point of view by considering the influence of class, the failure of attempts to relate supply to need is again clear. Perhaps this is most obvious in the continuing existence of the private sector, which perpetuates a system of medical care based on a principle in direct conflict with those of the National Health Service; that is, that priority be determined by ability to pay the price of treatment rather than by medical need.

The proportion of the population using the private sector is small, but is increasing, particularly in the hospital service which has always attracted more private patients than general practice. Most people having private hospital treatment insure with provident associations and it is on the figures provided by these bodies that estimates of the extent of private practice are largely based. There are two major organisations arranging insurance to cover the cost of private treatment, attracting between them 95 per cent of all provident subscription income, and in addition a number of local bodies. Subscribers may be individuals or members of group schemes which attract a discount and are linked to occupation. Group schemes often involve no contribution from the insured person, being organised by the employer as a fringe benefit. Schemes differ in the number of risks covered and in the provision made for dependants.[34]

The number of subscribers to the major schemes has multiplied over the years from 54,000 in 1948 to 883,000 in 1970. Subscription income has jumped over the same period from £127,000 to well over £17 million and benefits paid from £92,000 to nearly £15 million. Much of the growth reflects the expansion of group schemes, which increased by 44 per cent in the latter half of the 1960s compared with an increase of 18 per cent in individual subscriptions. Allowing for the small local schemes and for the fact that subscriptions cover on average two people, it is estimated that nearly two million persons were covered to some degree for private hospital treatment in 1970. They were very unrepresentative of the total population; three-quarters were from the upper and middle classes compared with one-eighth of the population as a whole, and over half of them were over fifty-five.

The provision of facilities within the hospital and specialist branch of the Health Service to meet this demand for private treatment is sanctioned by the National Health Service Act of 1946 and later legislation whereby the Secretary of State may authorise the setting aside of accommodation and services for paying patients. The number of private beds in Health Service hospitals has dropped slowly from 6647 in 1949 to 4350 in 1969, that is from just over to just under 1 per cent of all available beds. In addition, however, there are beds available in private nursing homes which remain outside the Health Service and their number has been increasing, though the total is not accurately known. Pay beds are unevenly distributed geographically in proportion to the population, there being nearly three times as many in the Metropolitan area as in the North-West.

Consultant status carries the prestige necessary for private-specialist practice, and until recently the majority of consultants had part-time appointments which allow the right to practise privately. The time spent on private patients, the numbers treated, and the fees received from them, however, are not known. Some indication of the value of private practice appears in the House of Commons report on National Health Service facilities for private patients. In his evidence a consultant surgeon estimated he earned about £5000 a year on the basis of one private operation a week while his part-time appointment meant he sacrificed about £800 of his Health Service salary.[35] In total the provident schemes paid £7.7 million in specialist fees in 1969[36] and, approaching the problem from yet another angle, Inland Revenue statistics for 1971 show 32 medical specialists earning between £15,000 and £20,000.[37] Since the Health Service was introduced the number of consultants having part-time appointments has risen from 5169 in 1965 to 5567 in 1970, but the figures represent a declining proportion of the total. In 1949 nearly 76 per cent of all consultants worked part-time but only 57 per cent in 1970.

The demand for and extent of private treatment in general practice seems much smaller than in the hospital service. Only about 5 per cent of subscribers to the provident associations insure for private G.P. costs and about 98 per cent of the population are registered as National Health Service patients.[38] So far as the G.P.s are concerned, between a quarter and a third have no private patients and the majority of those who do take them have less than 20. Probably 2 or 3 per cent of G.P.s at most rely entirely on private patients.[39]

The existence of the private sector inevitably raises questions about its effects on the public service, a matter which provokes much debate but about which relatively little is known. On the one hand are the supporters of the private system, who argue that its existence reduces the pressure on the Health Service, permits patients some choice in their consultant and in the time they are admitted to hospital, allows privacy for those who want it and, in attracting eminent specialists, sets and maintains high standards of medical practice which spread through the public service. On the other hand are those who oppose private medicine as based on market principles which are not appropriate for determining the distribution of medical care. The existence of the private sector, it is maintained, far from reducing pressure on the public service diverts resources which it urgently needs to private patients. Freedom of choice for those who can afford to indulge it, is counted of less importance than a distribution of medical care according to need. Furthermore, it is argued, the strength of public pressure to improve the public service is seriously reduced in so far as numbers of the more articulate, educated and politically powerful members of the community have no direct experience of it.

The Commons committee enquiring into facilities for private patients came to the conclusion that 'private practice operates to the overall benefit of the National Health Service',[40] and that no major changes to the system were needed – a remarkable finding in view of the amount of evidence to the contrary that it received. The nature of the evidence was admittedly inconclusive, largely representing the views or experiences of individuals, which were not quantified nor backed up by comprehensive research. But only prejudice can explain why the committee should give greater weight to the opinions of those who supported the private system than of those who criticised it.

Some of the criticisms, indeed, suggested serious problems in urgent need of further investigation, which make the committee's complacency hard to understand. Many witnesses pointed to the double standards within the Health Service with consultants concentrating on private patients and junior doctors attending to Health-Service cases.[41] Queue-jumping by private patients was said to be common,[42] and it was also alleged that sometimes Health-Service patients were deliberately made to wait longer than necessary in order to induce them to pay for their treatment.[43] The habit of using Health-Service equipment and staff for private patients was noted by many witnesses.[44] Moreover, criticism of such matters from within the Health Service tended, it was claimed, to be stifled because junior doctors relied on the goodwill of their seniors in obtaining senior posts themselves. Both the evidence for two standards of care and the allegations that Health-Service resources were exploited in the interests of private patients point to a negation of citizenship values.

There is also substantial evidence that professional people who use the Health Service do so more effectively than social classes IV and V. Middle-class patients seem to visit their doctors more often in relation to their needs, they tend to be referred more often for specialist treatment, and are more likely to be admitted to teaching hospitals than working-class patients.[45]

It is also clear that the distribution of resources as between different branches of medicine is very uneven. Failing attempts to estimate what an optimal distribution would be like, the significance of the inequalities cannot be precisely interpreted, but they nevertheless suggest substantial variations in the quality of care available for patients with different types of illness or disability.

An analysis of hospital beds shows approximately 40 per cent of the total for psychiatric and mentally-handicapped patients but only 11 per cent of consultants in mental health.[46] There is also a smaller proportion of award-holders in mental health: only 22 per cent compared with 70 per cent in cardiology and neurosurgery and 80 per cent in thoracic surgery. There is an even smaller proportion of geriatricians in relation to geriatric beds and fewer award-holders among them. Such glaring differences no doubt reflect other factors – such as the prestige attaching to different kinds of medical practice in the eyes of the doctors who distribute awards – besides the quality of care available for different groups of patients. It may even be true that fewer men of consultant status are needed for psychiatric patients and old people than for patients suffering from acute illnesses, but there is no evidence to support such a claim. And the distribution of awards, associated as it is with high professional status, must surely influence the choice younger doctors make about the area of medicine in which they practise.

The differences in the costs of beds for different types of patient again suggest a different quality of care. Figures for 1973 for the mentally ill showed weekly costs varying from £30 in non-teaching hospitals to £101 in London teaching hospitals. By contrast, a maternity bed cost £95 a week in a non-teaching hospital and £134 in a London teaching hospital, while a child's bed in a London teaching hospital cost £157.[47] Again, the significance of the figures cannot be exactly judged without precise calculations about the different requirements of different patients, but it is hardly likely that the low expenditure on hospital beds for the mentally ill represents a standard of care proportionate to their needs. Indeed, the very poor quality of a large part of the mental-health service is amply demonstrated by other evidence.[48]

Let us now examine the way in which health policies set out to tackle these problems. As we have seen, the National Health Service introduced in 1948 was designed to provide a comprehensive system of medical care available to everyone on the basis of medical need and without regard to economic position. In conception, then, the Health Service is thoroughly egalitarian; it invokes the principle of 'to each according to his need' and, being financed from general taxation, goes some way towards satisfying the other half of the socialist slogan. But in practice the ideals are very imperfectly realised. Standards of health vary between different social groups and different geographical areas and the amount and quality of provision also vary, but in association with circumstances which seem to have little to do with need. In so far as it is judged in terms of a system which aims to relate medical services to medical need, the National Health Service must be considered a failure.

The decision to abandon the market as a method of balancing demand and supply in medical care, as in anything else, has very important implications and if taken seriously would commit the government to comprehensive planning responsibilities. If supply is to be based on need, rather than being allowed to adjust itself to effective demand, then need must be defined and identified, attempts must be made to predict it and priorities must be settled. On the other side of the equation medical facilities, doctors, institutions and equipment must be organised to meet the need. Finally, services must be assessed and evaluated to see that they are effective, economical and of the desired quality. In practice, government planning in all these respects has been unsatisfactory and inadequate.

The first problem is to define those needs which are to be met. It is a problem because advances in medical science and the development of new techniques and new drugs make possible the treatment of a wide range of disabilities and diseases, but in many cases at very great cost. It would be unrealistic to suppose that all medical needs, in the sense of all those conditions which can be improved or controlled by medical treatment, can ever be met because the resources devoted to health purposes must always be limited. It therefore becomes necessary to decide what needs are to be recognised and how resources are to be distributed between them; in other words, objectives and priorities have to be established for the National Health Service.

In practice, little attempt has been made by the central department to define or measure health needs or to establish priorities to guide the distribution of resources between different branches of the service. As we have seen, available statistics are largely concerned with the use of health services and with mortality rates rather than with the incidence of sickness and disease.[49] In such a situation the Health Service responds to the most powerful demands made upon it, which may well work to the disadvantage of the more feeble and inarticulate patients. Failure to discover need is evident in the various studies which have shown a substantial amount of preventable and treatable disability among old people, for instance. This situation clearly offends against the idea that medical care should be available for all who require it; the Health Service has discarded the market as a means of distribution, but it has not developed a satisfactory alternative.[50]

The problems of identifying needs are difficult enough. The further question then arises as to what weight or priority is to be given to different claims on the service. This kind of decision is extremely complicated. If the aim is a distribution of medical care on citizenship principles without regard to power, wealth, status or to any circumstances other than need, how can the case of the powerless and the poor be effectively represented and how can their interests be guaranteed? An appeal to democratic decision-making pre-supposes that everyone is similarly capable of pleading his cause and it also pre-supposes some measure of agreement about the distribution of resources. Failing agreement, decisions based on a majority vote may still overlook the claims of minorities. But this is a fundamental problem of democratic government, and the Health Service is nowhere near the point at which it would be confronted with such basic issues. The machinery for testing popular opinion is extremely poorly developed, and the basic information about needs and effective methods of treating them, which would be necessary for rational decisions, is largely lacking.

The next question that arises when considering how far the Health Service is based on citizenship principles, concerns supply. How far are doctors, hospital beds and other medical resources distributed between different regions, classes, sexes, ages and illnesses in accordance with their respective needs? The information we have suggests that the distribution of health services and personnel reflects not so much considered judgement about needs and priorities but rather the interests and preferences of the medical profession. The power of the doctors in shaping the pattern of medical care is immense. When the National Health Service was established they were able to secure substantial representation on the various administrative bodies, particularly the hospital authorities and local executive councils. There is little attempt to assess or control the standards of medical practice, and doctors themselves have been very influential in determining not only the content of professional training but in defining future manpower requirements and hence the number of places provided for medical students. Furthermore it is the senior and established members of the profession who have the power to recognise and reward distinguished contributions to medicine through the distribution of merit awards.[51]

In this situation, and lacking firm direction from the central department, attention seems to have been concentrated on those areas of medicine that are professionally most interesting and rewarding while the less interesting and less rewarding branches have been neglected. And here is the dilemma, for there is no reason to suppose that the interests of doctors and the needs of patients or the opinion of the population about what should receive priority will coincide. Professional interests tend to be focused on the development of complicated surgical techniques and on curative medicine rather than on the care of the chronic sick. Lay opinion might prefer to give higher priority to the care of the increasing number of geriatric and psychiatric patients, though the order of preferences cannot be assumed.

This is not necessarily a criticism of the doctors for choosing the work which appeals to them, but rather a criticism of the planning authorities for failing to persuade doctors into those specialities and those regions which need them most. To some extent, of course, doctors will try to move into those branches of medicine, areas of the country and hospitals which carry high professional status or offer the best opportunities for private practice or for pursuing their own particular interests; hence the concentration of consultants and senior hospital doctors in teaching hospitals, in the Metropolitan region and in surgery and obstetrics, and their relative scarcity in non-teaching hospitals, in the North and South Wales and in geriatric and psychiatric medicine. The choice of career must also to some degree reflect the nature of medical education. The training of doctors has been severely criticised for its preoccupation with diseases which have little relevance to modern society and its failure to attend sufficiently to those illnesses associated with old age and mental disorder which are becoming increasingly prevalent.[52]

Apart from the questions of need, priorities and supply, a further problem is to find ways of assessing the quality and effectiveness of medical care. It has become very clear over recent years that in some branches of medicine, in some institutions and in some geographical areas the standard of provision is very bad. This has been dramatically demonstrated in the series of enquiries into allegations of ill-treatment and neglect in a number of long-stay hospitals, and it is also apparent from the reports of the Hospital Advisory Service, established in 1969 as a means of keeping a ministerial eye on such hospitals and of trying to encourage higher standards within them. The Advisory Service works through teams of doctors, hospital administrators, nurses and social workers who are appointed to visit and report on different groups of hospitals, and in the first instance attention has been concentrated on institutions for the mentally sub-normal, the mentally ill and geriatric and chronically-sick patients. Understandably enough, the new service found it necessary to proceed with caution. 'It has been essential to ensure that hospitals understood that the visit was intended to be helpful and on the basis of professionals advising professionals rather than detached experts coming to criticise.'[53] The reports from the different teams are at pains to refer to progressive planning and the development of new techniques in some regions, but the general tenor of the conclusions carries an overwhelming indictment not of the personnel but of the conditions in which they have to work.

> Nursing care in many hospitals is of a very high standard but, in far too many, nursing resources are so slight compared with the number of patients to be cared for that little more than basic care can be provided . . . . Many hospitals for the mentally handicapped are grossly overcrowded; fifty or more patients in wards intended for forty is a common finding. There is often no room for lockers or personal possessions, too few toilets and too few staff to give elementary training . . . . Many boards are still . . . refurbishing these (very large and isolated) old hospitals while making no attempt whatever to establish a more modern pattern of care, and . . . are failing to provide any services nearer to the patient's home. It is difficult to believe that such grossly distorted services would be accepted by any other branch of medicine.[54]

Comments on hospitals for the mentally ill are of a similar kind, though there is an additional problem that in a rapidly developing branch of medicine where methods of treatment are often uncertain and experimental, and where a new organisation of care based on district hospitals is developing, many hospitals and regional boards feel a lack of clear guidance from the central department as to how the new organisation can best be achieved.[55] The efforts of the hospital authorities to develop their psychiatric services and to link them to the local-authority services were very variable.

> Many of the psychiatric hospitals . . . [are] excessively large, sited very inconveniently to the populations they serve, and frequently so designed that modern therapeutic policies are frustrated . . . . Many make the development of anything approaching a normal community with some mixing of the sexes extremely difficult. Even worse, many contain excessively large wards, fifty, sixty or seventy beds being common. It is generally agreed that a ward of thirty patients is the maximum number a nursing team can care for effectively . . . . On wards of fifty or more patients which may be staffed by one or two nurses per shift, it is obviously impossible to develop effective therapeutic relationships.[56]

The report on the geriatric hospitals also draws a depressing picture of overcrowding, poor facilities, lack of staff and a substantial number of patients who do not need hospital care but who cannot be discharged because there is nowhere else for them to go. The overall judgement on all the various hospitals visited is a grave one. 'There can be little doubt that the three services I have been visiting have been the under-privileged part of the Hospital Service. Within them, however, there are enormous variations, some parts are very good indeed, but some fall well below an acceptable standard for a hospital service in 1970.'[57]

The Hospital Advisory Service is the first step towards trying to encourage higher standards of care; but it is limited to the long-stay geriatric and psychiatric hospitals, and during the first year all the hospitals visited contained between them only 12 per cent of National Health Service beds. The service will have to be greatly expanded if it is to keep a regular check on all Health-Service institutions and this is to ignore the other parts of the service. Professor Dollery has pointed out that there are two major difficulties in attempting to assess the quality of medical care: the first to persuade the medical professions that their work should be scrutinised, and the second to find ways of measuring their standards.[58] At present the profession has certain powers to control bad practice, but in fact it only intervenes in cases of gross negligence or professional incompetence. Professor Dollery urges an advisory service for the whole of the Health Service, 'a continuing external but professional evaluation of the performance of health services', and goes on to discuss how this might be organised.

Any attempt to assess quality must rest on sure methods of evaluating the effectiveness of different kinds of care and of different medical techniques. And this means an attempt to look not only at the supply and consumption of medical services – measures of standards that have been commonly used – but also at their 'outcome'. That is, there must be research to test the value and effectiveness of particular treatment programmes.[59] The task has an added urgency in an organisation like the National Health Service, which is insulated from market forces and from effective competition, and where an easy response to rising costs is to seek increasing funds from general taxation : 'A thorough re-appraisal of the existing systems for the finance and delivery of medical care . . . is now required. As part of this process, a review of the uses of information at all levels within the health services must be given the highest priority.'[60]

Over the past ten years or so a range of research projects has developed with the support of the D.H.S.S. aiming to measure needs and to evaluate services by testing the effectiveness of particular preventive and curative techniques and particular methods of organisation and record-keeping.[61] The account of activities sponsored by the D.H.S.S. is interesting, not only in its description of work in progress but also in its demonstration of major fields of enquiry which are yet barely touched and, very significantly, in the way it finds it necessary to justify its research activities.

> Some people have questioned the sense of searching for unrecognised need when the National Health Service has difficulty in coping with the need it does recognise. There are two ripostes to this. First, research on unrecognised need in the Department's programme is more than balanced by research in inefficient use of resources. Secondly, it is likely that some unrecognised need is more important than some need that is already met . . . . It is increasingly accepted that . . . health services will be unable to do everything that is technically feasible . . . . Knowledge of total need and therefore studies of need will be necessary for the establishment of rational priorities.[62]

A different way of trying to control standards of medical practice is to establish effective methods of dealing with complaints from patients. The making of complaints has always been a difficult business in relation to the Hospital Service, and an ombudsman has recently been appointed for the Health Service whose job will be to deal with patients' complaints.[63] The value of the appointment, however, is very doubtful as the job is to be done by the parliamentary commissioner on a part-time basis, and complaints are to be investigated in the first instance by the relevant local health authority. As Professor Abel-Smith has pointed out, hospital authorities cannot be relied upon to conduct thorough investigations; patients or staff may be victimised and evidence may be suppressed.[64]

If the National Health Service is to be assessed as an attempt to match medical care to medical need then its most serious failure has been the lack of any effective planning machinery to identify needs, establish priorities, distribute available resources accordingly, and assess standards of care. The two most important pressures which govern supply are not need,[65] but demand – not necessarily backed up by economic power, though all the more forceful when it is – in the form of articulate requests for attention, and the interests of the medical profession. Nevertheless it is the structural problems of the Health Service which pre-occupy the government, and both Labour and Conservative proposals for change have emphasised above all the importance of a unified administration to replace the tripartite system.

The concentration of responsibility for all health services in one local authority rather than three, and the establishment of a clear chain of command from the central department through the regions to the local area boards no doubt facilitates planning and research but it in no way guarantees it. The new structure will only benefit patients if the commitment to enquiry into need and evaluation of standards continues and expands. The Conservative document, in particular, which stresses managerial efficiency but pays little attention to problems of defining aims and objectives, holds out little hope in this respect.[66]

There is also a very obvious danger in the plans of both political parties in that both involve the removal of health services from local government and a corresponding reduction in democratic control. The nominated community health councils which are supposed to enable local people to express their views and criticisms are poor substitutes for the independent, elected representatives of local government. Not only is there a shift of power from the consumers to the bureaucracy but the powers and composition of the new authorities also suggest a shift in the relative influence of different elements in the medical profession, in favour of consultants and away from the G.P.s and community doctors. This is likely given the reduced powers of the area boards *vis-à-vis* the regional authorities, and the reduced representation of the local authority and profession at area level under the Conservative plans.[67]

It will need very determined planning to redress the shift in the balance of power towards consultants and away from G.P.s, and in favour of professional and bureaucratic rather than lay and democratic control. Indeed the possibilities of a democratic ordering of priorities within the health services seem more remote under the new plans than before.

NOTES

1. There are a number of notifiable diseases which should be reported to the local health authorities, but notification is generally regarded as partial and incomplete.

2. See Ethel Shanas *et al.*, *Old People in Three Industrial Societies* (Routledge & Kegan Paul, 1968) with reference to the dangers of relying on people's own assessments of their medical condition.

3. See, for example, C. T. Dollery, 'The Quality of Health Care', in *Challenges for Change*, ed. Gordon McLachlan (Oxford University Press, 1971); Brian Abel-Smith, 'Public Expenditure on the Social Services', *Social Trends*, no. 1 (1970); A. J. Culyer, R. J. Lavers and Alan Williams, 'Health Indicators', in *Social Indicators and Social Policy*, ed. Andrew Shonfield and Stella Shaw (Heinemann, 1972).

4. The mortality rate for a given sex or social class is expressed as a percentage of the rate for both sexes and all classes.

5. In the *Decennial Supplement, England and Wales, 1961* (H.M.S.O., 1971) the Registrar-General claims that it is impossible to disentangle real changes in the death rates of the different classes from apparent changes due to changes in the classification of occupations.

6. *Trends in British Society*, ed. Halsey, table 11.19.

7. Ibid. table 11.10.

8. Registrar-General, *Decennial Supplement, England and Wales, 1961, Occupational Mortality Tables*.

9. B. E. Coates and E. M. Rawstrom, *Regional Variations in Britain* (Batsford, 1971) pp. 227 ff.

10. C. A. Moser and Wolf Scott, *British Towns* (Oliver & Boyd, 1961) appendix B.

11. Office of Population Censuses and Surveys, *The General Household Survey*, Introductory Report (H.M.S.O., 1973) table 8.10.

12. Ibid. table 8.13.

13. Ibid. tables 8.15 and 8.16.

14. Ibid. table 8.26.

15. Ibid. table 8.3.

16. *Trends in British Society*, ed. Halsey, table 11.17.

17. The consulting rates for different classes expressed as a percentage of the rate for all classes.

18. *Trends in British Society*, table 11.18.

19. *The General Household Survey*, table 8.36.

20. Ibid. table 8.34.

21. Moser and Scott, *British Towns*, appendix B.

22. D.H.S.S., *Hospital Costing Returns for 1973* (H.M.S.O.,

1973). The cost of a hospital bed is, of course, a very inadequate guide to the quality of medical care, but nevertheless the variations are suggestive.

23. D.H.S.S., *Annual Report 1972*, Cmnd. 5352 (H.M.S.O., 1973) p. 180.

24. Coates and Rawstrom, *Regional Variations*, p. 182.

25. House of Commons, Fourth Report from the Expenditure Committee, Session 1971–2, *National Health Service Facilities for Private Patients* (H.M.S.O., 1972) appendix 8.

26. D.H.S.S., *Annual Report 1972*, p. 181.

27. *National Health Service Facilities for Private Patients*, Memorandum by the Department of Health and Social Security, appendix 11, p. 5.

28. Rosemary Stevens, *Medical Practice in Modern England* (Yale, 1966) part IV.

29. *Trends in British Society*, ed. Halsey, table 11.37.

30. Coates and Rawstrom, *Regional Variations*, pp. 197 *et seq.*

31. Ibid. pp. 207–8.

32. Ministry of Health, *Health and Welfare*, Cmnd. 3022 (H.M.S.O., 1966).

33. They have been examined by Bleddyn Davies for a range of welfare services in *Social Needs and Resources in Local Services*.

34. Michael Lee, *Opting out of the N.H.S.* (P.E.P., 1971) p. 12.

35. *National Health Service Facilities for Private Patients*, p. xiii. A maximum part-time consultant accepts the obligations of a full-time post but is paid only nine-elevenths of the whole-time salary in exchange for the right to practise privately.

36. Lee, *Opting out of the N.H.S.*, p. 18.

37. Inland Revenue Statistics, 1971, quoted in *National Health Service Facilities for Private Patients*, p. xiii.

38. Lee, *Opting Out of the N.H.S.*, p. 7.

39. Samuel Mencher, *Private Practice in Britain* (Bell, 1967) pp. 16, 17. Professor Mencher collected measures of the extent of private practice from a variety of sources.

40. *National Health Service Facilities for Private Patients*, p. xxii

41. Ibid. appendices 33, 46, 50, 54.

42. Ibid. appendices 34, 57, 61.

43. Ibid. appendices 38, 47.

44. Ibid. appendices 22, 34, 38, 45, 46, 47, 48, 54, 55, 58.

45. R. M. Titmuss, *Essays on the Welfare State*, 2nd ed. (Allen & Unwin, 1963) 'Appendix to Lectures on the National Health Service in England'.

46. D.H.S.S., *Annual Report 1970*, Cmnd. 4714 (H.M.S.O., 1971) table 59 and p. 226.

47. D.H.S.S., *Hospital Costing Returns*.

48. See pp. 85–6, for a discussion of the Reports of the Hospital Advisory Service.

49. Rosemary Stevens, *Medical Practice in Modern England* (Yale

University Press, 1966); Abel-Smith, 'Public Expenditure on the Social Services'; Halsey (ed.), *Trends in British Society*, chap. 11.

50. The range of information and the type of data needed to make proper assessments of need are discussed by K. Bispham, Susan Thorne and W. W. Holland, 'Information for Area Health Planning', in *Challenges for Change*, ed. McLachlan.

51. There are four grades of award worth £6330, £4800, £2820 and £1200 a year respectively in 1971. *National Health Service Facilities for Private Patients*, appendix 64.

52. See Thomas McKeown, *Medicine in Modern Society* (Allen & Unwin, 1965); *Report of the Royal Commission of Medical Education, 1965–68*, Cmnd. 3569 (H.M.S.O., 1968).

53. *Annual Report of the Hospital Advisory Service, 1969–70* (H.M.S.O., 1971) p. 6.

54. Ibid. paras 36, 45 and 46.

55. Ibid. para. 64.

56. Ibid. para. 70.

57. Ibid. para. 105.

58. C. T. Dollery, 'The Quality of Health Care', in *Challenges for Change*, ed. McLachlan.

59. Peter Draper, 'Some Technical Solutions for Planning for Health', *Journal of Social Policy*, vol. 1, part 2 (April 1972).

60. J. R. Ashford, 'The Uses of Information within the Health Services. The Challenge of Technical Change', in *Challenges for Change*, p. 132.

61. See the report on current research from the D.H.S.S. in Gordon McLachlan (ed.), *Portfolio for Health* (Oxford University Press, 1971).

62. G. K. Matthews, 'Measuring Need and Evaluating Services', in ibid. Also Andrew Shonfield and Stella Shaw (eds), *Social Indicators and Social Policy* (Heinemann, 1972) chap. 6, for a discussion of the problems involved in trying to measure medical need and changes in standards of health.

63. See Brian Abel-Smith, 'A Hospital Ombudsman?', *New Society* (22 April 1971) for a discussion of the case for such an appointment. See also *Report on Hospital Complaints Procedures* (Davies Report) (H.M.S.O., 1973).

64. Brian Abel-Smith, 'Ombudsman' in *New Society* (2 March 1972).

65. 'A need for medical care exists when an individual has an illness or disability for which there is effective and acceptable treatment or care.' Ibid. p. 28.

66. D.H.S.S., *National Health Service Reorganisation*, Consultative Document (May 1971).

67. Brain Abel-Smith, 'The Politics of Health', *New Society* (29 July 1971).

CHAPTER 6

The Distribution of Education

It is only during the past twenty or thirty years that education has become accepted as a crucial aspect of social policy. The welfare services associated with education, school meals, the school medical service and provision for handicapped children, have always had their place, albeit a small one, in studies of social administration and the welfare state. But analysis of the total education system, of how many children of what kind have what sort of education and for how long, is a relatively new interest. The change is indicative of a different definition of the subject. Social administration can be concerned mainly with public services for the relief of destitution and for the care of the more obvious physical and mental disabilities, but it is also concerned with inequality and with those institutions, public and private, which significantly influence men's standards and styles of life. Once this is recognised the importance of education is obvious. The effect of different kinds of school on different kinds of children, the relative part played by schools, families and the wider social background in education, and the very different advantages enjoyed by children from different classes or different geographical areas, then become matters of great significance. For it can be shown that education is systematically related to social structure. It is both determined by and itself a determinant of a man's social, economic and political position.

The distribution of goods, services and opportunities stems primarily, of course, from the productive system. In agricultural societies the possession of land is the most important determinant of living standards and in traditional industrial societies land is replaced by capital. Income, wealth and political power then become a matter of a man's work situation or, more broadly, his relation to the labour and capital markets, and education is not an important determinant of opportunities. The educational experience of most children reflects the social position of their families, which in turn is determined by occupation and wealth. Thus, the early moves in the development of the welfare state were both towards public provision for failures, accidents and misfortunes which prevented employment, and also towards more positive measures to provide healthy living and working conditions.

In the more advanced industrial societies the situation is now very different. Changes in production methods, in technology and in the choices and preferences of consumers mean a constant demand for new skills and a constant threat of obsolescence for old skills. The relation between education and occupation becomes close and complicated and educational systems become increasingly significant in the distribution of 'life-chances' to a degree which, at least in principle, is independent of classes, ethnic groups or families.[1]

This is not to deny the dominance of the market in social distribution. At the same time, however, educational qualifications of different kinds become essential for an increasingly wide range of jobs. In a technologically advanced society education can be considered as a special form of capital.[2] It is not surprising that it has become an important object of social policy in the twentieth century, absorbing 5 to 7 per cent of the G.N.P. of most countries and an increasing proportion of government social spending. Moreover, investment in education may be regarded as important not only for industrial modernisation and economic growth but also in relation to the social rights of citizens.

In Britain, as elsewhere, the education system is the outcome of a unique combination of social and economic circumstances. But it has two features which are common to other countries of North-West Europe. First, the state has acted to abolish the typical nineteenth-century division between primary and secondary education for the middle and upper classes, which led to universities and professional careers, and elementary education for everyone else, which led to manual work and unskilled occupations. Second, there has been an expansion of higher education. Both these trends bring the European arrangements closer to the American, moving in the direction of more equality of educational opportunity and towards universal higher education.

Important differences remain however. In Europe the move to comprehensive secondary education, which began much earlier in the United States, has been slow to develop. In Britain the first half of the twentieth century saw the development of a scholarship system to admit poor children to the secondary grammar schools, while those who were not successful in the examination remained in the elementary schools, which by 1944 had developed a variety of forms. The Education Act of 1944 abolished elementary education for the working classes and substituted primary and secondary stages for all children. But in practice there remained internal divisions at the secondary level between grammar, technical and secondary-modern schools. The comprehensive movement, still incomplete, has been a phenomenon of the post-war years.

Britain too, unlike the United States, has retained a private sector in education, varying in expense and quality but led by a famous group of public schools which take children at thirteen and which traditionally have close links with Oxford and Cambridge. In the long run private schooling has been declining, though there are signs that the trend is beginning to change. Just under 7 per cent of all children go to private schools, but the fact that those children make up over 15 per cent of all who stay beyond the statutory leaving age is some measure of their special position.

How far do the educational arrangements in this country forward the cause of equality of opportunity? To answer this question we must establish the importance of other institutions – particularly the family and the market – in providing education, and analyse the effects of government policies, both on the supply of education and on the demand for it among different social groups in the population. An examination of the statistics reveals the very wide differences in the chances for education of children in different schools, in different parts of the country and from different family backgrounds.

In 1971 there were 7,666,000 children aged 5–15 in school. 5 per cent were in independent or direct-grant schools and the remainder in one or other of the variety of establishments maintained by local education authorities. 43 per cent of children in local-authority secondary schools were in the old secondary moderns, though by 1971 there were nearly as many, 36 per cent, in comprehensives. Only a small minority, 15 per cent, were in grammar or technical schools.[3] There are marked differences in the proportion of children from different schools staying beyond the statutory leaving age; 33 per cent of children in local-authority schools were still there at 16 but only 6 per cent at 18, compared with 75 per cent and 15 per cent of the same ages in the independent schools. Only 16 per cent of all children over 15 remained at school, and of those staying on 16 per cent were in independent and direct-grant schools, 32 per cent in maintained-grammar or technical schools, 30 per cent in comprehensive and 16 per cent in secondary-modern schools. Thus, chances of education beyond 15 are greatest for children who are educated privately and slightest for those in secondary-modern schools.

The statistics, as well as common knowledge, suggest that the quality of education varies in the different institutions. A higher proportion of graduate teachers is to be found in grammar than in modern or comprehensive schools, and in direct-grant than in maintained schools.[4] There are notable differences in the number of children per teacher, which varies from 19 or more in local-authority modern and 17 in local-authority grammar schools, to 11 in independent secondary schools (see Table 6.1, p. 95).

Geography also affects children's chances of staying at school after 15 and the quality of the education they receive. More children stay

TABLE 6.1

Pupil/teacher ratios: regional analysis, January 1971, England and Wales

	North	Yorkshire and Humberside	East Midlands	East Anglia	Greater London	Other South-East	South-West	West Midlands	North-West	Wales	England and Wales
Schools maintained by Local Education Authorities											
All primary schools	27·0	26·9	27·4	25·6	25·8	27·0	26·8	27·7	28·1	25·0	26·9
Secondary schools											
Middle-deemed secondary	23·0	22·7	—	—	21·7	21·6	19·0	23·0	21·6	18·6	22·3
Modern	19·7	19·6	18·9	18·6	18·3	18·6	19·2	19·2	19·1	19·6	19·0
Grammar	17·8	16·8	16·6	16·6	15·9	16·3	16·9	16·5	16·9	18·0	16·7
Technical	16·9	17·2	15·4	18·2	16·9	16·5	17·0	16·5	16·9	—	16·6
Comprehensive	17·9	17·8	18·1	17·2	16·6	17·7	17·7	17·5	17·7	17·8	17·5
All other secondary	18·0	18·8	18·8	18·0	16·7	17·9	18·2	17·7	17·4	18·9	17·7
All secondary schools	18·6	18·4	18·1	17·8	16·9	17·8	18·2	18·0	18·2	18·3	17·9
All maintained schools	22·7	22·5	22·7	21·9	21·0	22·3	22·5	22·7	23·1	21·7	22·3
Direct-grant schools											
Grammar	16·9	16·7	17·0	15·9	15·8	15·7	16·5	16·3	16·9	14·7	16·4
All direct-grant schools	15·7	15·7	16·1	15·7	15·5	13·6	15·5	14·1	16·2	14·1	15·4
Independent schools recognised as efficient											
Primary	12·3	14·5	13·5	12·3	15·6	12·3	11·2	13·0	16·4	15·4	13·2
Secondary	11·2	11·0	11·8	12·0	13·1	10·9	9·9	10·4	13·8	10·7	11·1
All recognised independent schools	13·5	13·1	13·0	12·7	14·3	12·3	11·4	12·6	15·9	13·5	12·8
Other independent schools											
Primary	12·6	15·6	14·9	13·0	15·0	13·8	13·5	16·0	16·6	15·7	14·6
Secondary	13·8	12·0	6·8	9·4	11·5	10·3	10·7	—	12·0	13·7	11·1
All other independent schools	13·7	14·6	13·7	12·8	14·0	13·5	13·1	15·1	15·3	15·0	13·9
All schools	22·2	22·1	22·1	21·0	20·3	20·8	20·9	22·1	22·5	21·4	21·4

SOURCE: D.E.S., *Statistics of Education 1971*, vol. 1.

TABLE 6.2

Proportion of pupils remaining at school until age 16 and 18 by region, maintained schools (excluding special schools) only, 1950, 1961, 1971, England and Wales (percentages)

		1950 Boys	1950 Girls	1961 Boys	1961 Girls	1971 Boys	1971 Girls
North	until 16	9	9	16	14	28	27
	until 18	2	1	4	3	6	5
Yorkshire and Humberside	until 16	11	11	20	17	31	29
	until 18	2	1	4	3	7	5
East Midlands	until 16	11	10	19	16	29	27
	until 18	2	1	5	3	6	4
East Anglia	until 16	9	9	16	15	27	27
	until 18	2	1	4	2	6	4
South-East	until 16	14	14	28	24	40	39
	until 18	3	2	6	4	8	6
South-West	until 16	13	12	22	20	34	33
	until 18	2	2	5	3	6	4
West Midlands	until 16	9	9	19	17	30	29
	until 18	2	1	4	3	6	5
North-West	until 16	10	10	19	17	28	28
	until 18	2	1	4	3	5	6
Wales	until 16	17	19	26	26	35	37
	until 18	5	3	8	5	9	7
England and Wales	until 16	12	12	22	20	33	33
	until 18	3	2	5	3	7	5

NOTE: The percentages are calculated by expressing the numbers in schools aged 16 and 18 as percentages of the pupils aged 13 in the schools 3 and 5 years earlier. The percentages are somewhat overstated if there has been a net inward migration, and understated if there has been a net outward migration, to or from the areas shown.

SOURCES: Halsey (ed.), *Trends in British Society*, table 6.16; *Statistics of Education 1971*, vol. 1.

longer at school in the South-East and Wales and the early leavers are concentrated in East Anglia and the North-West (see Table 6.2). This tendency is associated with the substantially higher proportion of grammar-school places provided in Wales in the past, though the recent move towards comprehensive education has absorbed many of the former grammar schools. In 1936 31 per cent of 13-year-olds in Wales were in grammar schools, compared with 20 per cent in England. Table 6.3 (p. 97) shows the different proportions of children in different

TABLE 6.3

Percentage of 13-year-old pupils in schools and streams of various types by area, 1968 and 1971, England and Wales

Area	Modern		Technical		Comprehensive		Other secondary		Grammar		Direct grant		Independent	
	1968	1971	1968	1971	1968	1971	1968	1971	1968	1971	1968	1971	1968	1971
North	51	43	2	1	17	40	11	2	17	13	1	1	1	1
Yorkshire and Humberside	49	33	2	1	24	50	6	4	17	12	2	2	—	—
East Midlands	50	41	1	1	22	32	8	9	18	16	1	1	—	1
East Anglia	76	57	1	1	3	25	1	2	18	14	1	1	1	1
Greater London	37	27	2	2	31	44	11	10	18	15	1	1	1	1
Other South East	55	42	3	2	13	38	11	4	17	14	1	1	1	1
South West	55	46	1	1	23	33	1	3	18	16	1	1	1	—
West Midlands	60	47	2	1	13	31	7	5	17	15	—	—	—	—
North West	57	48	2	1	17	29	1	2	17	15	5	4	1	1
Wales	34	26	—	—	44	58	3	3	18	13	—	—	—	—
England and Wales	51	40	2	1	20	38	7	4	17	14	2	1	1	1
England														
Counties	59	48	1	1	13	32	6	2	19	16	1	1	1	1
County Boroughs	48	36	3	1	24	43	7	6	15	12	2	2	1	—
Total	53	41	2	1	19	37	7	5	17	14	2	2	1	1
Wales														
Counties	41	33	—	—	33	47	4	4	22	16	—	—	—	—
County Boroughs	13	2	1	—	78	94	—	1	8	2	—	—	—	—
Total	34	26	—	—	44	58	3	3	18	13	—	—	—	—
England and Wales														
Counties	58	47	1	1	14	33	6	2	19	16	1	1	1	1
County Boroughs	47	35	3	1	27	45	7	6	14	11	2	2	1	—
Total	51	40	2	1	20	38	7	4	17	14	2	1	1	1

SOURCES: Statistics of Education 1971, vol.I; and Halsey (ed.), Trends in British Society.

types of school in different areas in 1968 and 1971. Wales and the South are relatively well supplied, and the North and North-West relatively badly, with graduate teachers, and the number of pupils to teachers in these two areas is above and below average respectively (see Table 6.3, p. 97).

The proportion of children from different schools and from different areas going on to further education is shown in Tables 6.4 and 6.5 (p. 99). The direct-grant and independent schools send the largest proportion of their pupils to universities or other institutions, followed by the maintained grammar schools; more children from Wales than from England go on to higher education, more from the South of England than from the North, and more girls than boys.

The association between education and social class is well established. Children from the professional and managerial classes have a better chance of going to grammar schools and universities than those from the manual-worker classes, and the difference is most marked at the extremes. Comparing children of different generations, it may be seen that substantially more of those born in the late 1930s than of those born before 1910 had a grammar-school education, though the differential chances of the different social classes remained much the same.[5] Further analysis of the group of children born in the late 1930s shows the proportion of children from different social classes in grammar schools at different ages and clearly illustrates the educational differences between children from different social backgrounds.[6] Over 40 per cent

TABLE 6.4

Destination of school-leavers by type of school attended, 1970–1, England and Wales (per cent of all leavers)

Type of school	Employment[a]			Full-time further education		
	Boys	Girls	Boys and girls	Boys	Girls	Boys and girls
Grammar	55	47	51	45	53	49
Secondary Modern	92	88	90	9	12	10
Comprehensive	87	83	85	13	17	15
Other secondary	84	81	83	16	19	17
All maintained	84	79	81	.16	21	19
Direct Grant	37	34	35	64	66	65
Independent	42	38	40	58	63	60
All schools	81	76	78	20	24	22

[a] Including temporary employment before entering full-time further education, other destinations and destinations not known.

SOURCE: *Statistics of Education 1971*, vol. 2.

TABLE 6.5

Proportion of all school-leavers going on to some form of full-time further education, by region, 1970–1, England and Wales (percentages)

Region	Boys	Girls	Total
North	16·4	21·5	18·9
Yorkshire and Humberside	16·2	22·3	19·1
East Midlands	20·7	24·5	22·5
East Anglia	22·3	25·4	23·8
Greater London	17·0	19·4	18·2
Other South-East	21·8	26·3	24·0
South-West	24·4	28·0	26·1
West Midlands	16·8	24·9	20·7
North-West	19·3	23·3	21·3
Wales	23·5	29·1	26·2
England	19·3	23·8	21·5
England and Wales	19·5	24·1	21·8

SOURCE: *Statistics of Education 1971*, vol. 2.

of the children of professional and managerial families were still in grammar schools when they were 17 compared with 10 per cent of all children and less than 2 per cent of those of unskilled workers. A recent study of education authorities in the North-East region has suggested that high social class is significantly and positively correlated and low social class significantly and negatively correlated with expenditure on secondary schooling.[7]

Looking at it in another way, the proportion of all children leaving school at 17 in 1960–1 with at least two 'A'-level passes, the minimum requirement for university entry, diminishes with social class and is smaller among girls than among boys for all classes.[8] If the qualifications of school-leavers are analysed by both parental occupation and type of school attended, the relation between social background and achievement appears in more detail, and it also becomes clear that the direct-grant and independent schools have a very much better record than the maintained schools.[9] An examination of the social background of boys in public schools shows the non-manual classes to be heavily over-represented while the manual classes are barely represented at all.[10] Furthermore, children in public schools do significantly better in their 'O'- and 'A'-level exams than children in maintained grammar schools, while the proportion awarded a university place is three times as great among the public-school pupils. Perhaps most striking is the success of these schools with children who had failed their 11-plus exams. Over 90 per cent of such children were successful with some 'O' levels, 35 per cent obtained one or more 'A' levels and 15 per cent were awarded a university place; by contrast 92 per cent of children in secondary-modern schools had no 'O' levels, none reached 'A' level and none was allotted a university place.[11] Class background may also be seen at work among children in maintained grammar schools. Those from social classes I *and* II are more likely to gain at least two 'O' levels even after poor 11-plus results than children from the manual classes.[12]

Similar influences govern the probability of entry to universities. Although a higher proportion of children from all social backgrounds now have a university education, the chances of those from unskilled backgrounds as compared with those from the professional classes have actually worsened.[13] It is the middle classes who have most effectively used the growing opportunities to go to universities,[14] and this is very significant with respect to the redistributional effect of public expenditure on education. It seems that educational services are markedly inegalitarian in their effects if not in their intentions.

The situation can be examined the other way round. A comparison of the social background of university entrants with that of the adult male population shows all the non-manual groups, particularly class I, to be over-represented among university entrants and all the manual classes, particularly class V, to be under-represented. The percentage of undergraduates drawn from the manual classes has barely changed since the 1930s and the proportion of male undergraduates actually fell slightly in 1961.[15] The small overall increase is due to a higher proportion of women coming from this kind of background.

It is clear, therefore, that the education system does not provide similar opportunities. In spite of the expansion of universities and the reorganisation of primary and secondary schools, children from different social classes and from different parts of the country are likely to have a different kind of educational experience. Family background and the expectations of teachers (the two are linked), are vitally important in determining both children's attitudes to school and their achievements. Educational reforms such as improving pupil–teacher ratios, building new schools and developing wider curricula may help, but they have only a limited effect. Failing more equality in incomes, jobs, housing and environment the schools in themselves can do relatively little to improve the children's educational experience.

Even though the power of an education system to bring about more equal chances for education may be limited, there are some policies which could mitigate the most obvious disadvantages and, by improving the quality of education for those who are presently worst served, relate supply more closely to need as opposed to demand. Two ideas are particularly important here: the notion of recurrent education and that of compensatory education.

The first policy would mean extending opportunities for education beyond the period of compulsory schooling. Time for study or for learning new trades or professions would be arranged through working life and would continue into retirement. Thus it would no longer be a minority but the whole of the population who proceeded to some form of further education. There are many arguments which can be marshalled in favour of such a policy. Some are linked to the special features of advanced industrial societies with their complex division of labour and rapidly changing methods and techniques of production. In such circumstances any education system, whatever its structure, must provide a wide variety of training in the skills needed to support the economy. The case for recurrent education rests on the desirability of spreading opportunities for training and education over all age groups. Under the present arrangements educational reforms benefit directly only those who are in or about to enter the schools and universities. The advantages of younger people so far as educational qualifications are concerned are easily demonstrated. There is an inverse relation between qualifications and age.[16]

Thus recurrent education would help to tackle the problem of redundancy which is inevitably associated with an economy based on changing scientific knowledge. It would also give older people a better chance to get to know and understand the changing and complicated society they live in, as well as to prepare themselves more effectively for their different activities in work, leisure and retirement. A system which provided continuing opportunities for training and education would greatly enhance individual freedom, in enabling men to make their own educational choices throughout their lives rather than requiring them to pass through a formal period of schooling which ends for the majority at 16. The idea of recurrent education is an important corollary of the principle of citizenship. It would work to reduce the inequalities imposed by a market system in mitigating disadvantages with regard to jobs and occupations where those disadvantages stemmed from age or from social background.

Equal opportunities for different generations would be one aim of an education system based on the idea of citizenship. Equal opportunities for children from different social classes would be another. The development of education for working-class children in the rich countries has been a response to the demand for an orderly and competent workforce and also, with the coming of democracy, to the desire of the working classes themselves for self-improvement and better opportunities. Formerly separate educational arrangements existed for the different classes, and to begin with the egalitarian challenge was met by enabling selected children to move from the one system to the other and, after the Second World War, by increasing the number of secondary-school places to provide for all children. Expansion has been evident in the universities too, and in Britain the number of places has been doubled in every decade since the 1940s, an expression of the widespread faith in education as a means to both individual and national prosperity.

This policy of extending opportunities for secondary schooling and further education reflects the liberal conception of equality. But liberal policies, emphasising opportunities and leading to expansion, failed even on their own terms. Opportunities for education in Britain have never been equal in different parts of the country, nor has the provision of better secondary schools and more university places during the 1950s substantially altered the relative chances of children from poor homes of going on to some form of higher education. As we have seen the proportion of all students from different social backgrounds remained much the same in the early 1960s as it was in the 1930s.

An alternative interpretation of equality is to emphasise not only equal opportunities to go to schools and universities but also equal opportunities to benefit from whatever they provide. This could never mean, of course, that all individuals would reach the same level of achievement; but it would mean that children from different social, economic and ethnic groups would have similar chances of receiving a particular type of education.

In this sense of bringing about equal opportunities to succeed, liberal policies have also conspicuously failed. They failed because they did not recognise that family attitudes and social circumstances are just as important influences determining children's school performance as schools, teachers and curricula. Once the educational significance of family and social background is appreciated, it follows that policies intended to bring about equal opportunities for different kinds of educational experience must pay attention to a child's home environment as well as to his school.

The issue of the relation between social deprivation and educational attainment was raised in the Plowden Report and led that committee to propose two strategies to compensate for the educational disadvantages suffered by children in poor areas: positive discrimination in educational policy in favour of Education Priority Areas and the development of community schools. The committee also urged the development of nursery schools in priority areas, and eventually universally, as a means of giving children from poor homes an opportunity of becoming familiar with books and toys, and of learning through play and more formal teaching the accomplishments that middle-class children tend to develop through their normal experience of family life.[17] In these ways children living in areas defined as educationally deprived would have resources concentrated on them in an effort to make conditions better than those obtaining in the rest of the country, to counter the handicap imposed by their social and physical surroundings.

The programme of action research in E.P.A.s which followed the Plowden Report has demonstrated the value of a great variety of experiments, including different forms of pre-schooling, in improving the quality of education in areas where social conditions are bad and where children's attainment in school is relatively poor.[18] But experience with positive discrimination in E.P.A.s reveals new dimensions to the problems of how far this kind of approach is a means to greater equality in education. Again, it is a matter of how equality is to be defined and of the relative emphasis to be placed on the different possible aims of positive discrimination. Such a policy may be seen as a strategy which, in compensating for their initial disadvantages, allows children from poor homes and neighbourhoods to compete on more equal terms with children from middle-class homes and middle-class neighbourhoods for further education; in other words it is a more effective means to equal educational opportunities for clever children whatever their social or ethnic background.

There is, however, another definition of equality, which emphasises not so much the need to enable clever children from poor families to win places in universities, but rather the need to raise the quality of the educational experience of the majority of children, who, given the limited opportunities available for higher education, will leave their schools for manual work and probably live out their lives in the same kind of social, physical and economic environment as that into which they were born. This second objective implies a rather different conception of what an egalitarian educational policy would be like. It would stress not only that all children should have similar chances of doing well in their schools and universities, but that just as much care and attention should be given to the education of the less able as to the clever. The content of education would differ not in quality but in kind. The notion of equality, it would be argued, is very inadequately expressed in a system which aims at providing the same for everyone as with Beveridge's scheme for social security. Egalitarian principles are more fully realised through arrangements which treat unequal needs unequally.

This approach, of course, raises fundamental questions about the purpose of education. How much weight is to be attached to cultivating academic talent and ability, and how much to giving children the kind of experience which will best equip them to understand the circumstances of their lives and encourage them to meet and tackle more effectively the problems of the areas in which they live?

There are obvious dangers in arguing that education should be determined by a child's immediate environment. The objection may be made that schools which aim to fit children for life in depressed areas, only reinforce the disadvantages with which those children are born by making it all the more difficult for them to move to middle-class jobs with middle-class incomes in middle-class areas elsewhere. There are various answers to such objections. First, the nature of income distribution, employment and educational opportunities in Britain means that only a minority of children can hope to escape from E.P.A.s and social justice requires the best possible provision for those who will have to remain. Second, the education which would be appropriate for such children would not in fact reinforce existing disadvantages, for it would not be a matter of teaching acceptance of existing conditions but of provoking informed criticism and stimulating ideas which might eventually help to change them. Moreover to base education on the problems and concerns that children meet in their daily lives is the most effective way of awakening their interest and enthusiasm in learning, which can then be more easily directed to the more traditional subjects. Third, children should not be encouraged to abandon their communities and the brightest hope for wider reform lies in the development of effective political pressure from within these areas themselves.

Such strategies will not appeal to Marxists, and those who support them face a bitter dilemma. In a society where advantages and needs are very unevenly distributed truly egalitarian policies are those which distinguish between people's circumstances and treat different needs differently. The attempt to provide a special kind of education for poor children in poor areas, in so far as it in fact leads to pressure for change may also lead to conflict if those with power and authority refuse to accede to the demands of the poor for a larger share in national resources. The outcome of E.P.A. and community-development policies is still uncertain; they may be abandoned and forgotten or they may lead to political confrontation and violence. Those who have faith in them as a way to greater equality without revolution hope that they will improve the lives of the people who live in the deprived and depressed areas and, at the same time, by spreading knowledge of their problems and demonstrating ways of tackling them, arouse a sufficient degree of public interest and concern to support effective measures for wider changes.[19]

NOTES

1. Education systems become not only significant in the distribution of opportunities but also, as centres of research, influential in economic growth and therefore in determining the total amount of wealth and opportunities available for distribution.

2. See Meade, *Efficiency, Equality and the Ownership of Property.*

3. D.E.S., *Statistics of Education 1971*, vol. 1 (H.M.S.O., 1972).

4. Halsey (ed.), *Trends in British Society*, table 6.14.

5. Ibid. table 6.21.

6. Ibid. table 6.22.

7. D. S. Byrne and W. Williamson, 'Some Inter-Regional Variations in Educational Provision and their Bearings upon Educational Attainment – The Case of the North-East', *Sociology*, vol. 6, no. 1 (1972) pp. 71–86.

8. Halsey (ed.), *Trends in British Society*, table 6.23.

9. Ibid. table 6.24.

10. Ibid. table 6.25.

11. Ibid. table 6.26.

12. Ibid. table 6.27.

13. Ibid. table 6.28.

14. There is a marked correlation between social background and educational attainment for children of similar measured intelligence. Of the most intelligent children, with an I.Q. of over 130, born in 1940–1, twice as many from the non-manual as from the manual classes took a university degree. For the less-clever children the differences were even more pronounced. Ibid. table 6.29.

15. Ibid. tables 6.20 and 6.31.

16. *The General Household Survey*, table 7.15.

17. The government later accepted the case for a great expansion of nursery-school places to provide for 90 per cent of four-year-olds and 50 per cent of three-year-olds over a ten-year period. In the first few years priority was to be given to authorities with 'substantial areas of social deprivation'. D.E.S., *Education : A Framework for Expansion*, Cmnd. 5174 (H.M.S.O., 1972).

18. A. H. Halsey, *Educational Priority*, vol. 1 (H.M.S.O., 1972).

19. See A. H. Halsey 'Government Against Poverty', in *Poverty, Inequality and Class Structure*, ed. Dorothy Wedderburn (Cambridge University Press, 1974).

CHAPTER 7

The Distribution of Housing

The distribution of houses, unlike health and education, is largely determined by the market. Most people buy or rent their dwellings privately, and the arrangements they make are only indirectly and occasionally affected by government policy. The minority who rent their houses from the public authorities have in the past had their rent subsidised, mainly by government subsidies payable to local authorities in respect of the houses they build, in some cases by local rates and in some cases through differential rent or rebate schemes. Government intervention has taken the form of a succession of largely unco-ordinated activities designed to control or regulate the free market and to encourage public authorities to build houses, and the outcome is frequently confusion and muddle in people's minds about their housing prospects and rights.[1]

These arrangements are now in process of change. Recent legislation, though in part temporarily suspended, requires local authorities to raise the rents of all their houses to an economic level and to subsidise only those tenants who can demonstrate their need. Thus market principles are being strengthened in the public sector in that tenants will normally be expected to meet the economic cost of their accommodation and help will be restricted to the poor. However, the private sector escapes any similar or consistent application of the principle of selectivity. Tenants of private landlords will also be faced with a fair rent[2] and will only be eligible for a housing allowance if their income in relation to their needs falls below a defined level, but people buying their own houses on mortgage will continue to receive financial help through tax relief on interest payments on the money they borrow without any enquiry into their resources. Indeed, the higher the income and the higher the marginal rate of tax, the larger the gain from tax relief.

Under the arrangements for housing allowances and rebates it is possible for rent liability to be reduced to zero just as, for families dependent on supplementary benefit, housing costs may be fully met by the Supplementary Benefits Commission. But houses are never supplied on the basis of an assessment of need and without charge, as happens with medical care and with education. By contrast with a hospital bed or a school place, a free house is a very rare thing; and any reduction in the economic rent depends on poverty and on an application by the tenant to the relevant authority which is followed by careful enquiry into resources.[3] The quality, size and amenity of the houses people live in vary more directly with income than the sort of education or medical care they receive. Geography as well as class affects the availability of houses as population growth or movement outstrips the supply in some areas and releases a surplus in others, but income is overwhelmingly important.

The reluctance of governments to intervene in housing to the same degree as in health or education is something which has to be explained. Accounts of the development of housing policy tend to pay attention, naturally enough, to what occurred rather than to what did not occur. But the continuing and increasing emphasis on houses as a private rather than a public responsibility at a time when the reverse is true in other areas of social policy calls for comment.

One reason for this relative neglect may be the difficulty of turning housing into a political issue once standards are high enough to avoid risks to the health of either their inhabitants or the rest of the community. A glance at the development of housing legislation makes it obvious that the main objects of the public authorities have been to replace dwellings that were structurally unsound, to clear the slums and to prevent overcrowding : to deal, that is, with conditions which might undermine physical health or moral character.[4]

Health and education, however, are more directly related to a country's efficiency, to the national interest and to individual opportunities, and are thus more likely targets for political action from the more powerful pressure groups. While bad housing conditions have been and are frequently cited as a contributory cause of social breakdown and disorder, in Great Britain, at any rate until recently, there has been relatively little of the racial or religious discrimination and antagonism that has exacerbated and emphasised the problem in, for instance, the United States and Northern Ireland, and the houses people live in remain largely their own concern.

Nor has the private character of the supply and demand for houses been challenged by professional interests. The development of collective responsibility for medical care owes much to the agitation of doctors for more resources and better conditions both for their patients and themselves. But the professions associated with housing have not used their power to try to bring about more government intervention in order to relate supply more effectively to need. Although officials and professionals make decisions about housing need, their judgements tend to reflect a conception of minimum standards if they are working in the public sector and are governed by what the market will stand if they are in private practice, and have little to do with citizenship principles. The strength of private interest is very great. Roughly 50 per cent of householders are owner-occupiers and private landlords rent dwellings to another 15 per cent. Neither of these groups is going to be very anxious for more public responsibility for or control of housing. At the same time the minority of households living in the million or so seriously unfit houses are unlikely to form an effective pressure group; many of them are old or poor or both.

There is another contrast with health in that the cost of a house is within easier reach of the average man, is more predictable and admits more individual choice than medical treatment. Sickness is much more difficult to anticipate than the need for a dwelling, and in any case, as the cost of medical care escalates with the discovery of new drugs and new techniques, it becomes impossible for medicine to remain a private matter where individuals pay for their own treatment; some kind of collective provision has to be organised. For all these reasons housing may appear as a less urgent matter for public responsibility than either health or education.

In 1970 there were 18,731,000 dwellings and rather fewer private households in Great Britain, excluding persons living in institutions. Over 95 per cent of the total population lived in private households.[5] In England and Wales in 1966 the average dwelling contained five rooms and the average family three people. More than half of all households lived at a density of between half and one person to a room, roughly

TABLE 7.1

Unfit dwellings by region, 1971, England and Wales

Unfit dwellings

Region	No. (thousands)	Per cent of all unfit dwellings	Per cent of all dwellings in areas
North Yorkshire, Humberside and North-West	540	43	10
South-East	231	19	4
Rest of England and Wales	473	38	8
England and Wales	1244	100	7

SOURCE: Department of the Environment, *House Condition Survey, 1971.*

a third had less than half a person to a room and 5 per cent more than one.[6] Seven per cent of all households shared dwellings.

It was estimated in 1971 that there were 1,244,000 unfit dwellings in England and Wales (see Table 7.1, p. 108) but apart from their structural condition houses vary in their amenities. In 1966 only 72 per cent of all households had the exclusive use of three standard amenities – fixed bath, hot-water tap and inside W.C. – and only 19 per cent of sharing households possessed all three. Figures for 1971 show 17 per cent of dwellings without one or more amenity, 12 per cent with no inside lavatory and 10 per cent with no fixed bath (see Table 7.2).

TABLE 7.2

Dwellings without exclusive use of basic amenities, 1971, England and Wales

Amenities missing	Per cent dwellings
Internal W.C.	12
Fixed bath	10
Wash basin	12
Hot and cold water at 3 points	14
One or more	17

SOURCE: *House Condition Survey, 1971.*

At the end of 1971, 50 per cent of dwellings in Great Britain were owner-occupied, 31 per cent were rented from a local authority or New Town and 14 per cent were privately rented.[7] More than 24,000 people in England and Wales were homeless.[8]

This is the overall picture of the housing situation at the beginning of the 1970s, but structural condition, amenities and density of occupation vary substantially in different parts of the country and according to social class. Geographically it is the Greater London area which, as might be expected of an area of high immigration, is the worst off in terms of overcrowding, poor amenities and shared dwellings.[9] Sharing in Greater London is more than three times as common as in England and Wales as a whole.[10] Regional differences in overcrowding and amenity are less startling and although conditions are worst in Greater London the areas with the best conditions vary. The East and South-West have the lowest density of occupation; London and the South-East, the South-West and the North are best off for amenity. It is a different matter so far as structural condition is concerned; here the South-East is very much better off than the North and other areas of England and Wales (see Table 7.1, p. 108).

The way in which the quality of housing varies with social class is easily demonstrated. The statistics show the relation between the income of the head of the household and amenities, between income and tenure, and the variation in standards between the different tenure groups. As would be expected, housing standards rise with income. According to *The General Household Survey* less than 1 per cent of the highest income group (over £40 a week) were without a bath or shower but 25 per cent of the poorest (less than £7.50 per week). Only 1 per cent of the top compared with 22 per cent of the bottom group had an outside W.C. and 73 per cent of the richest compared with 15 per cent of the poorest households had central heating.[11]

There is much more information about housing conditions in relation to tenure but its significance in terms of class differences rests on the association between income and tenure. This is clear enough.[12] In 1971 the median income for owner-occupiers with a mortgage lay in the £31 to £35 a week range, the highest for all tenure groups, compared with a median for all household heads of between £21 and £25 and of £12.50 to £15 for private tenants renting unfurnished. Council tenants had a median income of between £16 and £20. At the same time, 28 per cent of owner-occupiers with mortgages had incomes of over £40 a week but only 4 per cent of private renters and 3 per cent of council tenants.[13]

Thus owner-occupiers tend to have the highest incomes, and also the houses they live in tend to be the most expensive.[14] If tenure is related to age of dwelling it seems that more than half the houses built before 1919 are owner-occupied and over one-third are rented privately; only a handful are council houses (see Table 7.3, p. 111). Houses built after 1919 show a different pattern, with public authorities monopolising the renting sector and the tenants of private landlords dwindling to insignificant proportions, especially after 1945. Fewer of the most modern dwellings, only 44 per cent, are owned by their occupiers. Put in a different way, 68 per cent of privately rented unfurnished dwellings date from before 1919 and 8 per cent were built after 1945, compared with 4 per cent pre-1919 and 65 per cent post-1945 council houses, and 22 per cent of owner-occupiers with mortgages in the older houses and 48 per cent in the newer. The outright owners live in older houses – 46 per cent in those built before 1919 and 21 per cent in those built after 1945.[15]

Age alone, however, is no certain indication of quality; tenure is also very significant. Although it is true that council houses, which are younger than either of the other two groups, contain the smallest proportion of unfit dwellings and have the highest standard of amenity, there are significant differences on both these counts between owner-occupied and privately rented accommodation. In 1971, 23 per cent of the relatively small proportion of all dwellings that were rented privately were unfit, but only 4 per cent of owner-occupied houses, which were three times more numerous (see Table 7.3, p. 111). Unfit

TABLE 7.3

Dwellings by age, tenure and condition, 1971, England and Wales

Age	Owner-occupied		Rented from local authorities or New Town		Other tenures		All tenures	
	thousands	per cent	thousands	per cent	thousands	per cent	thousands	per cent
Before 1919								
Unfit	345	4	50	1	634	23	1202[a]	7
Fit	2742	30	126	3	1335	47	4364[a]	26
Total	3087	34	176	4	1969	70	5566[a]	33
1919–71								
Unfit	10	0·1	8	0·2	11	0·4	42[a]	0·3
Fit	5965	66	4599	96	841	30	11492[a]	67
Total	5975	66	4607	96	852	30	11534[a]	68
Total unfit	355	4	58	1	645	23	1244[a]	7
Total fit	8707	96	4725	99	2176	77	15856[a]	93
Total dwellings	9062	100	4783	100	2821	100	17100[a]	100

[a] The figure is not the sum for the row because the relatively small number of vacant and closed dwellings is omitted.

SOURCE: *House Condition Survey, 1971*.

houses are thus concentrated in the privately rented sector and it is also this group that has the poorest standard of amenity. In 1966 only 35 per cent had exclusive use of hot-water tap, fixed bath and inside W.C. compared with 81 per cent of owner-occupiers and 88 per cent of council tenants.[16] The overall position seemed to have improved slightly by 1971 but the relatively poor amenities in the private-rented houses remained (see Table 7.4).

TABLE 7.4

Lack of basic amenities by tenure, 1971, England and Wales
(percentages)

Amenities missing	Owner-occupied	Rented from local authority or New Town	Other	All
Inside W.C.	8	6	31	12
Fixed bath.	6	2	30	10
Wash basin	7	7	33	12
Sink	0·3	0·2	1	0·5
Hot and cold water at 3 points	8	8	37	14
One or more of above amenities missing	11	11	40	17

SOURCE: *House Condition Survey, 1971.*

The differences between tenure groups also emerge clearly from *The General Household Survey*. 9 per cent of all households had no bath or shower in 1971 but 12 per cent of those renting privately and 38 per cent in privately rented furnished accommodation were without compared with 2 per cent of council tenants and 6 per cent of owner-occupiers.[17] The pattern for other amenities is similar, with owner-occupiers on mortgage tending to be better off than those owning their houses outright, though the relative advantages of unfurnished as opposed to furnished tenants vary.

Finally, privately rented accommodation, especially the furnished sector, is more crowded than owner-occupied property. 8 per cent of unfurnished and 20 per cent of furnished tenants were living below the bedroom standard,[18] compared with 4 per cent of owner-occupiers and 10 per cent, a surprisingly high proportion, of council tenants. At the other extreme, just over half the households in unfurnished accommodation and only one-quarter of furnished tenants had bedrooms to spare compared with 72 per cent of owner-occupiers.

Although income and geographical location are the most important determinants of housing quality, standards also vary with family type and the colour of the occupants. 31 per cent of large families[19] lived below the bedroom standard in 1971 compared with 7 per cent of all households,[20] though they fared rather better than average in respect of amenities. Single or small households, especially where the householder is over sixty, were worse off for amenities.[21] Coloured were more crowded than white households: 23 per cent lived below the bedroom standard compared with 6 per cent of white households where the head was born in the United Kingdom and 11 per cent where he was born abroad,[22] although the relative crowding was associated with the larger average size of coloured households. Sharing amenities was more common among coloured households: 21 per cent and 25 per cent shared bath and lavatory respectively compared with 2 per cent and 3 per cent of whites with heads born in the United Kingdom and 7 per cent and 8 per cent of those with heads born elsewhere who were sharers.[23]

In summary, owner-occupiers, the richer half of the population, tend to live in houses that are more expensive, relatively spacious and have good amenities. Council tenants, who are rather below average earners, also have good amenities and only a very small proportion of their dwellings are unfit, though they are relatively crowded. Tenants renting privately, among whom are the poorest families, have the highest proportion of unfit dwellings, amenities are relatively poor and families are relatively crowded, particularly in the furnished sector. Households that are large, coloured or consist of single elderly people tend to be relatively badly off. As might be expected, there are fewer owner-occupiers and more private renters in Greater London, where housing conditions are particularly bad, than in the rest of the country. The highest rates of owner-occupation are in Wales, in the South-West and in the South-East outside Greater London.[24]

How is this situation affected by government action? Intervention in housing has been tentative. As it became clear that private building could not supply houses which were cheap enough for the poor to buy or to rent, the government developed two methods to try to ensure a supply of low-cost dwellings. Rents of private houses were controlled to protect tenants from rising costs; and local authorities, and in some cases private builders, were encouraged to build with the assistance of government subsidies to keep rents low. Local authorities were also at various times obliged or permitted to subsidise the rents of their houses by a grant from their own rate fund.

These attempts to influence, though not control, the building of houses have been only partially successful. Policies of enforcing minimum standards and at the same time controlling rents have led to a rapid decline in the number of private dwellings to rent and a deterioration in their quality. This lack of adequate and cheap accommodation has not been made good by the public sector. Many local authorities do not or cannot meet the local need for houses and there is no certainty that needs are in any case adequately measured. In some areas the problems are so intractable as to appear to defy solution by any localised and specialised agencies.

In assessing the effectiveness of public policies a number of matters are relevant: the extent of public as opposed to private building programmes, the arrangements for repairing and improving older property, the way in which tenants are selected for houses that are publicly owned, and the amount of financial assistance with housing costs that the government makes available in different ways.

As we already know, the majority of houses are supplied by private enterprise, now generally for sale rather than to rent. There was hardly any local-authority building before 1919 and during the years between the wars nearly three times as many houses were built privately as by local authorities. Immediately after the Second World War private building was strictly controlled and the majority of houses were constructed by public authorities, but in the later fifties this policy was reversed and since 1960 private builders have again become the main suppliers.[25] In 1971 local authorities built only 55,000 out of the 222,000 dwellings completed, and this was a smaller proportion than the year before.[26] Only just over one-quarter of the present stock of dwellings in England and Wales has been built and is controlled by public authorities.

The local councils are responsible for the maintenance of the houses they own and, as we have seen, their dwellings are on the whole in good condition and have a high standard of amenity. Privately owned houses, particularly those that are rented, are another matter. The age of the buildings means that repairs are more costly and conversions to improve the standard of amenity more necessary; at the same time rent controls, first introduced in 1919, have meant that it has often been uneconomic for landlords to maintain their property in accordance with current standards. Rent control is partly responsible for the virtual disappearance of privately built houses to let, as investment in houses to rent became increasingly unattractive in comparison with other forms of investment.[27] There has been a growing tendency for landlords owning rented accommodation to sell it and at the same time the quality of the privately held stock has declined. Since 1919 the number of privately let dwellings has halved and now represents only about a fifth of the total stock while the number of owner-occupied houses has increased eightfold.[28]

The effects of rent control are quoted by Stone. In 1964 the median yearly rent for private unfurnished dwellings was £54 for England and Wales, varying from £38 in the North to £77 in East Anglia and the South-East; at the same time, the economic rent for a two-bedroomed dwelling of approved standard even outside London would have been over £400.[29] Although the private property would be below the officially approved standard, Stone argues that the difference would not be so great as the difference in rents might suggest; there is little doubt that rent control has resulted in rents much below the economic level.

Rent controls thus discouraged private investment in houses to rent. Without subsidies or rents held below the economic level by controls, however, the poorest families could only afford sub-standard accommodation. Stone calculates that roughly 10 per cent of all households would need to pay over 30 per cent of total household income in rent if they were to meet the economic cost of an appropriately sized dwelling of adequate standard. Compared with recent experience this represents a very large amount: if the different tenure groups are distinguished, average rents for local-authority and private tenants amounted to 8 per cent and 9 per cent of total household income respectively in 1967, while mortgage payments were on average 11 per cent of the household income of owner-occupiers.[30] Only households with a very high income would be expected to devote 30 per cent of it to housing.

It is in an attempt to guarantee adequate standards for all families at prices they can afford that governments have introduced various subsidies as well as measures to control or de-control rents. In general both major parties share the aim of a sufficient supply of houses of an adequate standard; they differ in the priority they accord to houses among other possible objects of government expenditure and they have tended to disagree over the most effective methods of achieving their aims. The Labour party has been particularly concerned to control the cost of existing dwellings and to encourage local-authority building, while the Conservatives have put more faith in private enterprise to supply shortages and have been more ready to offer incentives to private builders.

Improvement grants are available for both local-authority and privately owned property and by 1969 grants had been approved in respect of over one million dwellings. The great majority were privately owned and of these two-thirds to three-quarters were owner-occupied.[31] Yet poor standards of accommodation are heavily concentrated in the privately rented sector.[32]

The outcome of successive policies is very unsatisfactory. As we have seen, there are over one million dwellings classified as structurally unfit and the number appears to have increased over the years.[33] Nearly one-quarter of all households lack one or the other of the standard amenities, and the proportion of households sharing dwellings actually increased between 1961 and 1966, particularly in Greater London and the South-East Lancashire conurbation.

Public policies are not calculated to solve the housing problem. Aims and objectives are not clearly defined and no reliable techniques have been developed for measuring need or adjusting the supply of houses to meet it. No system of priorities has been evolved which would ensure that houses would be available for persons in the greatest housing need and that those unable to afford the cost would be subsidised. Local authorities are permitted a great deal of autonomy in assessing local needs and planning their building programmes, and the central department does little to concentrate aid in those areas which have to tackle the severest problems.

It is through the subsidy arrangements that the government has tried to influence local-authority building. These have varied greatly since they were first introduced immediately after the First World War and have been radically revised under the Housing Finance Act of 1972. After the Second World War exchequer subsidies were available for building for 'general needs', but in 1956 they were restricted to building for slum clearance and to one-bedroomed dwellings. In 1961 there was an important change in that subsidies were adjusted to some extent to the needs of the area; poor areas, where potential rent income was below housing expenditure, receiving a subsidy three times as big as that available for richer districts. Another change was introduced in 1967 when subsidies were related to the total costs of new dwellings and designed to protect local authorities from fluctuating loan charges, the amount of subsidy being the difference between the cost of charge payable at 4 per cent and the cost of charges at the rate of interest that the local authority actually paid over the preceding year. In 1972 the Housing Finance Act changed the situation yet again by drastically reducing exchequer subsidies while requiring local authorities to raise the rents of their houses to an economic level.

In the past subsidies have only applied to houses built after the relevant Act was passed, so that the total amount of exchequer subsidy received by a local authority depended on the legislation under which its houses were built. The time of building also affects the costs which local authorities incur in another way. Councils which built mainly before the Second World War when costs were low and money cheap are much better off than councils whose major building programmes have been in more recent years when building costs and loan charges have been relatively high. Building costs also, of course, are affected by the price of land, which varies considerably between different authorities. The result is that exchequer subsidies have covered a higher or lower proportion of local-authority housing costs, depending not s much on the needs of the authorities concerned but on the historical circumstances – the legislation in force, the price of money, the cost of land – in which they carried out their major building programmes.[34]

Miss Nevitt shows how a combination of such factors could result in the highly anomalous situation where the neighbouring London boroughs of Chelsea and Fulham received during 1962–3 exchequer subsidies of 12s 1d and 6s 3d respectively for each pound of debt charges.[35] As Miss Nevitt points out, if need for housing subsidy were measured against the income of each authority, the degree of over-crowding and so on, Fulham's need would have been much the greater. A further result of this kind of situation has been a marked variation in the rents which local authorities have charged for similar houses. By charging current rents for old property, councils could lower the rents of new dwellings. Chelsea with a relatively high exchequer subsidy charged an average rent of 22s 7d for its pre-war houses but Fulham, with a rather lower proportion of pre-war houses, a lower rate yield per person than Chelsea and a relatively low exchequer subsidy, charged an average rent of 34s 3d.

The inequitable outcome of past policies can easily be demonstrated in this way. But the major problem of housing is a present one and it is inmensely variable in different areas. It is determined by the amount and quality of the local housing stock in relation to local demand, which is itself affected by many factors including population growth either through natural increase or migration, the rate of household formation, economic circumstances and social expectations.

Population movements into the industrial conurbations, and parti-cularly into the London area, pose problems for those districts which are completely absent in other parts of the country. It seems particularly unrealistic to expect that a number of independent housing authorities, as in Greater London, should grapple simultaneously with the housing problems of their areas in the face of extreme scarcity of land and under pressure of virtually uncontrolled population movements. Ultimately housing programmes must be planned in relation to economic and industrial development and over very wide areas – perhaps on a national scale – if the supply of dwellings is to be related to the need for them. In the meantime one London borough is left with a waiting list of over 11,000 from which it re-houses only 300 a year![36] Some boroughs have closed their lists to new applicants, thus effectively obscuring the dimensions of their problems.

The central department recognises the special problems of particular areas to some extent. London and, since 1963, thirty-eight housing authorities outside the metropolis receive special help in dealing with slum clearance. But it has been help of a non-pecuniary kind involving mainly visits to the local authorities by central-department officials who discuss problems, offer advice, encourage larger programmes and point to the advantages of joint planning by neighbouring authorities and the use of industrialised building methods.[37]

Local authorities are largely free not only to assess the needs of their areas and draw up their housing programmes but also to choose their tenants and, until the recent Housing Finance Act, determine the rent they shall pay. Local councils have different views about the importance of housing as opposed to other local-government activities and about the priority that should be given to housing particular groups. In the past the local authorities have built largely for young families and the great majority of council houses have two or three bedrooms;[38] single-person households and very large families have tended to be overlooked and many authorities are reluctant to house irregular families, such as unmarried women with illegitimate children. The requirement of a number of years residence before a family may be housed or even admitted to the housing list is quite common, in spite of advice to the contrary from the central department, and means that recent immigrants, whatever their housing situation, may not qualify even for consideration for a council house. Before the Housing Finance Act, applicants might also have been effectively excluded from council houses by high rents. Only 40 per cent of housing authorities operated a differential rent scheme in 1964 and many of the schemes that existed would not have reduced rents sufficiently to bring council houses within the reach of the poorest families.[39]

Government policy towards private enterprise has been variable, but a period of restriction immediately after the war has given way to a period of encouragement dating from the mid-1950s and culminating in the lifting of rent controls in 1957.[40] This has resulted in a higher rate of building by private builders, but the problem of distribution remains unsolved since the building has been for sale and has had little effect on the acute needs of those in the worst housing conditions.

More recently housing policy has been designed to rationalise housing finance, at any rate in the council and privately rented sectors. Some kind of rationalisation was surely overdue. The anomalies of the system of public aid towards housing costs which existed before the Housing Finance Act of 1972 have been adequately described elsewhere.[41] The richest group in the population, those who have or can borrow capital to buy their own houses, received tax relief on the interest they paid on the money they borrowed, while council-house tenants had an average subsidy from exchequer and rates which was rather less valuable than the average tax relief to owner-occupiers.[42] Moreover the relative advantage of owner-occupiers had been increasing since 1968. On the other hand, tenants of private landlords, the group with the highest proportion of poorest households, had least chance of financial help from public sources unless they were so poor as to have an income below the supplementary benefit scale, and were unemployed, in which case they would probably receive a housing allowance from the Supplementary Benefits Commission.

A move to regulate private rents, decontrolled after the legislation of 1957, occurred in 1965 with the introduction of machinery for establishing fair rents in the private sector. Rents which had been decontrolled were frozen at their existing value, but tenants or landlords were free to appeal to the rent officer to fix a fair rent which was supposed to reflect the market value of the dwelling, assuming that supply and demand were in balance. In determining fair rents, rent officers were in practice guided by a number of considerations but mainly by the rents fixed for comparable dwellings, the levels of recently negotiated market rents, and calculations as to what rent would be required to give a fair return on capital. Fair rents have tended to be set at a level about 20 per cent below related market rents, though in areas of stress the reduction has averaged 40 per cent. Applications to the rent officers have come increasingly from landlords rather than from tenants and an increasing proportion of applications have resulted in rents being raised rather than lowered.[43] In 1971, 77 per cent of applications came from landlords and 84 per cent of rents were raised.

This intervention in the private market had some effect in curbing the increases in rents which were a response to severe housing shortage and, more significantly in later years, in allowing landlords a greater return on their property. But the possibility of renting privately still depended on there being an adequate supply of accommodation and on the ability to pay the price. No subsidies were available to those with low incomes. In 1971 the Conservatives published radical proposals for altering the basis of housing finances.[44] Fair rents were to be established for all dwellings, including council houses previously subsidised by the central department, and tenants of both council and private property who could not afford the new rents would be eligible for a rent allowance related to income, to family size and to the fair rent of their dwelling. The amount of the housing allowance was to be determined according to national scales and tenants would apply to the local authority for their grant. The expressed aim of Conservative policy was to concentrate help on the poorest families, to stop indiscriminate subsidies to all council tenants and to restrict government assistance to areas of special need. All who could not demonstrate their need in accordance with the national scale would have to pay the fair rent.

There are various important features of these proposals. Perhaps most notable from the point of view of the availability of housing assistance to different groups in the population is that the help for the relatively rich, in the form of tax relief on mortgage payments, remained, while the average and low earners had to face increased housing costs with the withdrawal of subsidies and the lifting of controls. The rationalisation of finances, in other words, takes place only within the renting sector. Here the two most significant facts will be the size of the increases as rents rise to an economic level, which is specially significant for council tenants, and the needs standard which governs the payment of housing allowances.

There are no firm estimates of the level to which rent will rise, though Stone's figures suggest the rents of private controlled dwellings will multiply. The needs scale is very low. It is set at £18.25 a week for man and wife, at which point a couple will be liable to pay 40 per cent of the fair rent of their house with increasing payments proportionate to additional income and decreasing payments as earnings fall.[45] The needs standard is increased by £2.75 for each dependent child. The supplementary-benefits scale of needs allows £10.65 for ordinary requirements for a married couple exclusive of rent so that, taking account of the rent which would have to be paid, a couple with £18.25 would finish with net resources very near the supplementary benefit level, a minimum standard designed only to meet the cost of essentials.

The means test to be applied for housing allowances is thus a very ungenerous one. It seems that under the proposals all except the very poor and the relatively rich, the owner-occupiers, will have to meet a substantial increase in housing costs, even taking into account the effect of the housing allowance. Furthermore, the new system employs a kind of selectivity which in many other areas of policy has been found to be to some degree self-defeating. Benefits which depend on a personal means test and individual applications are avoided by substantial numbers of people who are eligible. The conditions for grants require a declaration of poverty of a kind that many people find humiliating and unacceptable. Rent-rebate schemes introduced for council tenants in Greater London, when council rents were raised to a fair-rent level, and for private tenants in Birmingham by a special local Act, both failed to reach a substantial proportion of people who were eligible for them.[46]

If we analyse the housing situation in terms of citizenship principles where the distribution of dwellings would be based on the idea that everyone was entitled to a house of a conventionally acceptable standard of amenity, then the present situation falls far short of the ideal. In fact the distribution of houses reflects the distribution of wealth and income rather than of need. The larger houses, in good condition and with good amenities, tend to be owned and occupied by the richer 50 per cent of the population, who either own or have easy access to capital. For the average and low earners borrowing money to buy a house is a much more difficult matter, and they are obliged to rely mainly on the rented sector where the supply of decent dwellings of suitable size and in the appropriate places is grossly inadequate.[47]

At the extreme are those who have no dwellings at all and who are housed by the local authorities in so-called temporary accommodation. This group has grown over recent years[48] and the problem is particularly acute in Inner London, where the number of homeless people increased threefold between 1950 and 1970.[49] As Professor Greve points out, however, statistics are unreliable and reflect 'not so much the trend in homelessness but rather the trend in the provision of temporary accommodation', the degree to which services are known and the reputation they have, as well as the criterion of eligibility used by the local authorities. Greve noted a fear in some authorities that making admission too easy might stop families making the effort to find their own accommodation, and that as a result authorities used deterrent policies which constituted a form of rationing that had nothing to do with need.

Thus housing policy seems to reflect to a great extent the *laissez-faire* approach to welfare. Most people live in the kinds of houses they can afford and for a substantial minority these are of poor quality. Successive governments have intervened in the housing market to control rents, to encourage slum clearance and also to empower and assist local authorities to build for various categories of need. To this extent there have been gestures to the liberal approach in the offer of limited assistance and protection to those who cannot fend for themselves,[50] but the outcome of these activities has been to leave many families without any houses at all and many more in dwellings which fall far below currently acceptable standards of amenity.

In housing, as in other areas of policy, a socialist approach would require first and foremost adequate assessment of need and determination of priorities. Unequal treatment of similar need by different authorities offends against the idea of citizenship, or of social justice as Greve puts it.[51] Moreover, if the definition of need is arbitrary and unsatisfactory so far as homelessness is concerned, it is equally so in other branches of housing policy. Local authorities may give housing need relatively little weight in selecting tenants for their dwellings,[52] while in Sunderland at any rate tenants' preferences have little influence on decisions about clearance and rehousing programmes.[53] Dennis's study of Sunderland points to some of the fundamental issues which arise when political decision-making is substituted for the market system. In particular, how far are the claims of experts, officials, administrators or professionals to order other people's lives legitimate? And in what circumstances would the idea of citizenship mean that the people themselves would at least participate both in defining their needs and in deciding how they should be met? The question of people's preferences about the houses they want to live in arises in another context in relation to the different kinds of tenure. In 1971 the Conservatives spoke of the desirability of more choice as between buying and renting a dwelling. It would be an important responsibility of any policy informed by citizenship principles to find ways of extending the possibilities of such a choice to those who cannot at present exercise it.

NOTES

1. Lucy Syson and Michael Young, 'Poverty in Bethnal Green', in *Poverty Report 1974*, ed. Michael Young (Temple Smith, 1974).

2. The 'fair rent' should represent the market value of a dwelling supposing supply and demand to be in balance. See p. 119.

3. Or sometimes it depends on an occupation which carries with it a free house as a fringe benefit.

4. See such different authorities as Edwin Chadwick, *The Sanitary Conditions of the Labouring Population of Great Britain 1842*, ed. M. W. Flinn (Edinburgh University Press, 1965), and Alvin Schorr, *Slums and Social Insecurity* (Nelson, 1964) on the physical and moral dangers of bad housing.

5. Central Statistical Office, *Social Trends*, no. 2 (H.M.S.O., 1971).

6. Halsey (ed.), *Trends in British Society*, tables 10.3 and 10.4.

7. *Social Trends*, no. 3 (H.M.S.O., 1972) table 102.

8. Ibid. p. 140.

9. Halsey (ed.), *Trends in British Society*, tables 10.6, 10.8 and 10.19.

10. The figure of 24 per cent of households in shared dwellings in Greater London compares with 2 per cent in West Yorkshire and 7 per cent in the East and West and in Merseyside, the most- and least-favoured districts outside Greater London.

11. *The General Household Survey*, table 5.43.

12. Though there is a warning in *The General Household Survey* (p. 10) that income data must be interpreted cautiously because of the large proportion of non-residents.

13. Ibid. table 5.19.

14. The median gross value of owner-occupied dwellings was £100 to £119 in 1971 compared with £80 to £99 for council and £60 to £79 for privately rented houses. Ibid. table 5.16.

15. Ibid. table 5.11.

16. Halsey (ed.), *Trends in British Society*, table 10.23.

17. *The General Household Survey*, table 5.13.

18. This allows one bedroom for married couples, for single adults aged twenty-one, for two persons under twenty of the same sex or for two children under ten.

19. Defined for *The General Household Survey* purposes as those

with three or more children or those with three or more adults and two children.

20. *The General Household Survey*, table 5.26.

21. Ibid. table 5.42.

22. Ibid. table 5.46.

23. Ibid. table 5.48.

24. Halsey (ed.), *Trends in British Society*, table 10.21. See also *The General Household Survey*, table 5.14.

25. Halsey (ed.), *Trends in British Society*, table 10.24.

26. *Social Trends*, no. 3, table 106.

27. Adela Adam Nevitt, *Housing, Taxation and Subsidies* (Nelson, 1966). Miss Nevitt gives a useful analysis of the decline of the private landlord.

28. P. A. Stone, *Urban Development in Britain* (Cambridge University Press, 1970) chap. 15.

29. Ibid. p. 236.

30. Halsey (ed.), *Trends in British Society*, table 10.37.

31. Ibid. table 10.29. See also *Social Trends*, no. 3, table 110.

32. Stone has pointed to the urgency of diverting more resources to the maintenance and repair of old property. *Urban Development in Britain*, pp. 267–87.

33. In 1934, according to the slum-clearance programmes of the local authorities, there were less than 267,000 unfit dwellings. No exact comparison with present figures is possible as local definitions of 'unfit' are notoriously variable. Rising standards since the 1930s may well account for the apparent deterioration in the housing stock, though many new slums were presumably created over a forty-year period when relatively little was spent on maintaining older property – particularly in the privately rented sector.

34. Nevitt, *Housing, Taxation and Subsidies*, chap. 7.

35. Ibid. p. 97.

36. Ministry of Housing and Local Government, *Council Housing Purposes, Procedures and Priorities* (H.M.S.O., 1969) para. 165.

37. J. A. G. Griffith, *Central Departments and Local Authorities* (Allen & Unwin, 1966) p. 244.

38. Between 1945 and 1960, 88 per cent of houses built by local authorities has two or three bedrooms. By 1968 the proportion had dropped to 71 per cent and many more single-bedroomed dwellings were being built. During the whole period the proportion of two- and three-bedroomed dwellings among those built privately never dropped below 90 per cent. Halsey (ed.), *Trends in British Society*, table 10.30.

39. R. A. Parker, *The Rents of Council Houses* (Bell, 1967).

40. See Malcolm Joel Barnett, *The Politics of Legislation* (Weidenfeld & Nicolson, 1969) for an analysis of the developments leading to the Rent Act of 1957. The author is particularly critical of the failure to carry out any adequate research into the housing situation and the likely effects of de-control.

41. Nevitt, *Housing, Taxation and Subsidies*; J. B. Cullingworth, *English Housing Trends* (Bell, 1965).

42. *Social Trends*, no. 3, table 115.

43. *Report of the Committee of Enquiry into the Working of the Rent Acts*, Cmnd. 4609 (H.M.S.O., 1971). See also *Social Trends*, no. 3, tables 113, 114.

44. *Fair Deal for Housing*, Cmnd. 4728 (H.M.S.O., 1971).

45. See K. M. Spencer, 'The Housing Finance Act', *Social and Economic Administration*, vol. 7, no. 1 (January 1973), for an explanation of the rebate and allowance schemes. The rates quoted are those in force in 1973.

46. Audrey Harvey, in *Social Services for All?, Part 3*, Fabian Tract 384 (1968). C.P.A.G., *Poverty*, no. 22 (Spring 1972).

47. This remains true in spite of the government's expressed desire to bring about greater fairness between one citizen and another in the opportunities for choosing between buying or renting houses. See *Fair Deal for Housing*, p. 1.

48. Halsey (ed.), *Trends in British Society*, table 12.6, and *Social Trends*, no. 3.

49. John Greve *et al.*, *Homelessness in London* (Scottish Academic Press, 1971) p. 57.

50. And also, of course, to offer substantial assistance to those who can fend for themselves, that is the owner-occupiers.

51. Greve *et al.*, *Homelessness in London*, p. 268.

52. Ministry of Housing and Local Government, *Council Housing*.

53. Norman Dennis, *People and Planning* (Faber, 1970). See also J. G. Davies, *The Evangelistic Bureaucrat* (Tavistock, 1972).

CHAPTER 8

The Distribution of Welfare

In discussions of social administration and social work, welfare has come to have a special meaning. On the one hand it refers to services other than cash payments which are designed to meet some kind of social dependency or deviant behaviour; on the other hand, in the sense of 'welfare case', it refers to the situation of people who rely on, or are judged to need, or are constrained by such services. Thus in speaking of welfare we are concerned with the social care – as distinct from financial assistance, medical attention or education – available for those who are dependent on others for this kind of support in childhood or old age, or through some physical or mental handicap, and for those who offend against public norms of behaviour and respectability. For the most part the rearing of children and the care of the old and handicapped is a family matter. But the system of family support may break down, sometimes due to the separation or death of parents, sometimes because the family cannot or will not provide the skill or time demanded by an old or handicapped person, sometimes because standards of care fall below the level commonly regarded as acceptable.

Historically, failing family care, the support and care of the old, the sick, the halt and the lame, and of the children of the 'perishing and dangerous classes' has been mainly a matter for religious, philanthropic and charitable bodies. In the latter part of the nineteenth century the deliberate restriction of state help and the setting up of the workhouse, the harsh symbol of the deterrent Poor Law, left plenty of scope for voluntary effort which throve on the fruits of the economic prosperity of the time.[1] But industrialisation brought social and economic problems as well as wealth; and the aspirations of a gradually expanding electorate, the perhaps rather uncertain appeal of socialist slogans calling for equal rights and opportunities, the growing power of new professions concerned with various aspects of human welfare, and the desire to maintain law and order were all forces working for increased government intervention in the lives of individuals. The pressure for more collective responsibility gradually eroded the foundations of minimal state intervention on which the deterrent workhouses had been built, and could not be contained by the voluntary system. Thus, the legislation to do with children, the old, the handicapped and the delinquent reflects growing concern with *welfare* as well as with destitution, though, at the same time, those defined as able to do so might be required to pay for the services they received. In practice, however, the term 'welfare' often seems a misnomer, and the gestures towards classlessness which are to be seen in attempts to substitute need for financial poverty as the basis for receiving welfare help are largely defeated by class differences in income, power and ways of life. Very few old people from the professional or managerial classes are to be found in local-authority accommodation, much of which still carries the flavour of the workhouse, and proportionately few of the children of those groups are to be found in local-authority homes, foster homes or approved schools. Middle-class families are more likely to make their own arrangements or to buy the help they need privately.

How in fact is welfare distributed? How far do the arrangements we have reflect an egalitarian approach to social policy, and what would be required to make such an approach a reality? The public authorities, in this case local government, now have comprehensive powers to assist individuals and families in circumstances where they judge a need exists, and they may do this by arranging residential care or providing a variety of domiciliary services. In extreme cases where, for example, the care of children is grossly inadequate the local authority may take measures to remove a child from his family into its own care – compulsorily if necessary by obtaining a court order.

If we try to look at the quality and adequacy of the care provided through family and community and by public bodies, we are at once in difficulties. We have very little information about, and few means of judging, the standard of care provided privately or through the family. We know that far more handicapped and elderly people are cared for in their own homes than in institutions, and that far more people make their own arrangements than rely on local-authority domiciliary services. Welfare thus remains primarily a matter for the family but we know little about how satisfactorily it works. There is plenty of evidence, however, that public services are commonly insufficient and often of poor quality. Many of the poorest areas are the worst served in terms of staff and resources at the command of the personal social services. But attempts to assess the degree of inadequacy, or the amount of maldistribution as between different geographical areas or different social classes, are vitiated, as so often in social administration, by the lack of information about need against which the supply must be measured. Without comprehensive knowledge of need, statistics about the services have little significance.

The question is also complicated by the difficulty of measuring the results of social work. Services to do with material provisions have reasonably obvious aims and the impact of policies can be fairly clearly measured. Housing policies may be judged according to whether there are enough houses of a conventionally adequate standard which people actually want to live in and at prices they can afford to pay. We can probably assume that provision of domestic help, chiropody, hot meals, clubs and so on add something to the comfort of the old or the handicapped. But how is the effectiveness or quality of social work to be assessed? The aims of social or welfare work are nebulous; they are concerned with bringing about a state of affairs where an individual or family behaves in a way which is socially acceptable and with promoting 'welfare' and harmonious personal relationships. There are two problems here: first to measure how far the desired situation has been brought about, and second to decide how influential the social worker's activities have been in producing it.

The kind of indices which measure success in other types of professional activity have not been developed for social work. Advances in medical science may be seen in new techniques and drugs which control disease and probably influence to some degree the reduction in mortality rates, particularly infant mortality, and the increased expectation of life. But how can progress in social work be demonstrated? Delinquency rates, illegitimacy rates and other indices of social integration, even if they can be accurately established, do not provide satisfactory measures for they reflect much wider changes in social structure and social values; in so far as they could be considered an indication of the significance of social work they would suggest that it was increasingly ineffectual and perhaps damaging.[2]

Bearing in mind, then, the limited knowledge available we may turn to the evidence that exists about the extent and adequacy of the welfare services. Public spending on local welfare services for the old and the handicapped rose from 0.1 per cent of G.N.P. to 0.2 per cent between 1951 and 1968, but for child care the proportion remained constant at 0.1 per cent.[3] For both services however the amount of money spent more than doubled during the period – the increase being greatest for the local welfare services.[4] If we look at expenditure in money terms over a rather shorter period, we find an increase in the cost of local welfare services (excluding payments by recipients) from £19 million to £85½ million between 1958 and 1970.[5] Much of this increase will be accounted for by the increasing number of people in the age group. During the same period the number of people of 65 and over in the total population increased by nearly 40 per cent,[6] and the number of persons in institutions rose by over 50 per cent.[7] The apparent rise in costs is also accounted for partly by the fall in the value of money

Thus how much more is being spent per person, or how much more generous services have become, remains unclear.

There is little doubt that local-authority social-service departments now cast their nets more widely than ten years ago. Not only are there more old and handicapped people in institutions, but the number of handicapped people registered has increased markedly.[8] It is notorious that registration may carry with it little in the way of services. Nevertheless expenditure on handicapped people in the community, excluding the blind and the deaf, rose over the same period from £28,000 to £334,000. Again, in interpreting such statistics, allowances must be made for inflation. How far they represent a rise in the quality of services remains uncertain.

The number of children in local-authority care has also risen. In 1971 children's departments were responsible for 87,000 children compared with 63,000 in 1951, though the later figure includes 9000 children in remand homes and approved schools following the legislation of 1969.[9] The need for additional expenditure for the increased numbers would have been partly offset by the growth in the use of foster care – considerably cheaper than the institutions which were a more usual type of provision in the earlier years.

Put in a rather wider context, health and personal social services received 11 per cent of all public expenditure in 1971 compared with 12 per cent for education and 5 per cent for housing. Over the twenty preceding years education had almost doubled its share, while that of health and personal social services rose by only 1 per cent and the proportion for housing dropped.[10] Figures for public expenditure on health and personal social services break down the categories and show 11 per cent of the total going to the local-authority social services in 1971. The situation had barely changed since 1969, and comparison with earlier years is difficult as services then coming under local-authority health departments were transferred to the personal social services after 1968, but the local-authority services together had increased their share of the total by 4 per cent since 1951.[11]

Public services for old people are in some ways easier to assess than those for children, in so far as it is possible to get some idea of how far they are satisfying their clients, if not of how far they are meeting need. The evidence suggests that both institutional and domiciliary care is generally insufficient and often, particularly in the case of institutions, of very poor standard.[12] But public services play a very minor part in the lives of most old people. Less than 5 per cent are in any kind of institution, and there are few who receive any substantial assistance from the public domiciliary welfare services. In 1965 less than 2 per cent of married couples and 4 per cent of single men and single women had domestic help from local authorities;[13] a far higher proportion received unpaid domestic help, mostly from relatives. Unpaid assistance from local authorities was much less common and was concentrated on help with housework rather than with other matters such as shopping and the preparation of meals.[14] Less than 1 per cent of married couples and only marginally more single women and single men had meals brought to their homes (usually two a week) though for women and men living alone the proportions rose to 3 per cent and 6 per cent respectively. The great majority of old people depended on commercial laundries or unpaid help for washing; no married couples and only 1 per cent of single men and single women received local-authority help.

The government inquiry demonstrates the very small part that local authorities play in various important services, but we also have some evidence about how far needs are supplied from other sources. In 1962 Townsend and Wedderburn found that 4 per cent of their sample of old people received domestic help from local authorities but many more, 6 per cent, said they needed it. Nearly two-thirds of this latter group were moderately or severely incapacitated, one-third were childless and nearly as many were living entirely alone.[15] At the same time 1 per cent of old people were found to be receiving a hot meal in their own home at least once a week, but nearly six times as many would have liked the service. 7 per cent of old people were having chiropody treatment either from a voluntary or public service and 11 per cent paid for such a service privately; a further 11 per cent would have liked such attention. In addition a substantial number of people were handicapped by poor hearing or poor sight, but had no services or treatment for their disability, and others expressed a desire to see their G.P. more often (3.5 per cent of those in their own homes and 4 per cent of those in institutions). One-third of the sample were dissatisfied with their houses.

Apart from the overall inadequacy, standards of services for old people are very uneven geographically. Variations reflect not only differences in need but also the structure of local departments and the political colour of local councils.[16] There is ample evidence of disagreement in interpretations of need. As Miss Harris points out[17] the legislation is loosely worded; local authorities are required to provide residential accommodation, for instance, for those needing care or attention which would not otherwise be available and to provide domestic help for households where it is needed, but they themselves are left to make the definitions more precise, with very different results.

If, for example, we consider the provision of home helps. All authorities provide this service. But the circumstances in which this help is given, and the duties performed, vary between the authority which says that elderly people should be given, as far as possible, as much help as they need to keep their homes the way they would have kept them themselves had they been able, and the authority which rules that home helps should spend the minimum amount of time necessary to ensure that the rooms used exclusively by old people are kept in a sanitary condition. The first of these authorities would argue that seeing their homes sparkling and polished, with their knick-knacks dusted, has a big psychological effect – that their duty is not merely to keep old people going in their own homes for as long as possible, but to keep them happy in their homes. The second of these authorities argues that as the service is subsidised by public money, it should be kept to the bare essentials to prevent deterioration.[18]

It is also clear that the actual jobs done by home helps vary. While practically all do the normal cleaning work only about one-third of old people have help with their washing and fewer have help with ironing. As many as 3 per cent of the elderly who had considerable difficulty in getting their meals received no help with this from their domestic worker and only 14 per cent said their home helps ever prepared meals for them.[19]

The deficiencies in the service may arise because there are certain things home helps do not generally do, such as polishing and making beds, either through lack of time or because local authority rules limit their activities – they are not normally supposed to clean windows or paintwork or do gardening – or because over three-quarters of elderly people have only two or fewer visits a week and on the other days jobs are left undone.[20] The report from the Government Social Survey (*The Home Help Service*) estimates that to satisfy the unmet needs of existing recipients and to provide for all who are eligible but not presently receiving help, the size of the service would have to be increased two- or three-fold, and this estimate makes no allowance for more generous conditions of eligibility.[21]

Knowledge about the extent and nature of local-authority services for the physically handicapped is sketchy but again it is clear that the provision is very variable. In 1965–6 the number of persons registered ranged from 0.7 for every thousand persons in Cheshire to 10 in Hull; and in the same year average expenditure varied from £2 a head in Durham to £53 in Bristol.[22] An enquiry in 1970 into the situation of handicapped and impaired people revealed just over three million persons over 15 in private households who were so classified.[23] The people identified were grouped into different categories according to their disability and its effect on their capacity to lead normal lives. There emerged at one extreme 157,000 men and women considered to need special care and at the other nearly two million who were imparied but thought to need little or no support.

The study again demonstrates the minor role played by the local authorities in the lives of handicapped people. Only 220,000 persons were on local-authority registers of the handicapped in 1968, and 82 per cent of the impaired people questioned had never heard of such registers. Registration with a local authority is no guarantee of comprehensive services, but it carries a better chance of some kind of help. Two thousand of the very severely handicapped and 90,000 of those less impaired were living alone and receiving no welfare services. More than three-quarters of those who might have attended local-authority centres had never heard of such facilities.

A higher proportion of impaired people than of the whole population had low incomes and more of the severely disabled, obviously enough, were incapable of employment. A third of all impaired people were retired and a third were housewives. The proportion of those who worked increased as handicap lessened, and it was estimated that 554,000 were working, though one-third of them had limited capacity. Over a quarter of a million people under retirement age were permanently disabled and would never work again, though only a very small minority had never worked at all. More impaired persons than others were without qualifications, naturally enough as disability may interfere with education. Only 16 per cent of the few who had been registered with the Department of Employment thought that registration had helped them, and many more wanted a job in a sheltered workshop than were capable of doing one.

In general the housing of impaired, as of old, people is no worse and no better than that of the rest of the population. Some of the handicapped, however, need special modifications to their homes because of their disability. People on local-authority registers are more likely to have had some modification but only about a quarter of the sample had had any alterations to their houses. One-fifth would have liked some special arrangements – usually handrails or inside W.C.s. In all it was estimated that 200,000 households containing people with very severe or appreciable handicaps needed re-housing or some improvements to their accommodation.

The staffing situation for the old and the mentally and physically handicapped is poor. The Mallaby Committee[24] found that 5 per cent of posts for mental-welfare officers and 3 per cent for welfare officers had been vacant for more than six months. At the end of 1965 11 per cent of posts for mental-welfare officers were empty, and 40 per cent of mental-welfare officers and welfare officers for the old and handicapped in post had less than the desirable qualifications. Moreover it is doubtful how far local-authority establishments are in any case appropriate in relation to local needs. Sumner and Smith point to the wide-spread inadequacies in services for old people, to the very vague estimates that many local authorities have of the extent of need in their areas, and to their consequent inability to make accurate plans for meeting it.[25]

It is similarly difficult to assess children's services. Since the war the emphasis of provision has changed, with a marked shift away from institutions and an increase in both the number and proportion of children boarded out. There are now fewer children in residential nurseries and more in small, family-group-type homes.[26] How far the service at present meets the need for it is impossible to say, though there is plenty of evidence of local-authority departments being below establishment strength and lacking professionally qualified staff. In March 1966, 334 or 13 per cent of all established posts for child-care officers in local-authority departments were vacant and the Mallaby Committee found that 7 per cent of the posts in their sample had been vacant for six months or more. They also found that over 40 per cent of officers in post had less than the desirable qualifications in the local authorities' judgement. In more detailed terms this meant that 28 per cent of the officers were professionally qualified, 9 per cent were recognised by virtue of their experience, 23 per cent had a social-science qualification only and 40 per cent had no qualifications. Such a situation does not suggest services of a high standard. Nevertheless there does not yet exist any established way of identifying need which is independent of the work actually performed by local authorities and against which local-authority provision might be assessed. In so far as attempts have been made to measure need little significant correlation has been found with the supply.[27] In a recent enquiry into variations in services for children, Bleddyn Davies points to widely differing standards, and discusses possible ways of developing more equitable arrangements which would require the central department to control more closely the distribution of resources and personnel and the development of research and evaluative techniques by the local authorities.[28]

Thus the personal welfare services are beset with problems. They are generally inadequate even to cope with the demands made to the local authorities; they are often of poor quality; they are very unevenly spread geographically; and the variations in supply appear to be largely unrelated to variations in need. Reliable estimates of need are as lacking now as when the Younghusband Committee reported in 1959,[29] and techniques of measurement remain undeveloped. Further, there are criticisms, which have mounted over the years since the war, of the organisation of the personal social services. On the one hand, divided administrative responsibility has emphasised problems of unco-ordinated policies and lack of co-operation between workers. On the other hand, increasing attention is now being paid to the relation between social-service departments and the people they serve. How much do people know about the services supposed to be provided for them and how easily can they reach them? How far does the kind of service that is supplied reflect what people actually want? This latter question raises major issues, which have to be settled for the whole range of social provision, of how far consumers' wishes and preferences are to be regarded as criteria for determining the supply and evaluating the quality of public services, and of how far local democratic institutions permit the exercise of power and expression of opinion by local populations.

Let us now consider the implications of the idea of citizenship for the planning and organisation of personal welfare services, in order to see how far the present arrangements reflect or deny egalitarian principles. One of the most important elements in a system of welfare services based on the notion of citizenship would be a distribution of resources determined by judgements about needs and about priorities among them. But whose judgements about need are they to be? If political decisions are substituted for the free choices of individuals which define 'need' in an ideal, and non-existent, free-market situation, then those decisions are in practice made by a variety of officials, administrators and professionals employed in the public services and influenced, in a democratic system, by the wishes and preferences of consumers and laymen. A perfect democracy, however, is just as elusive as a perfect market. British political institutions have not guaranteed that the public services reflect or are sensitive to the needs or wishes of the people for whom they are intended. This is not only a matter of a failure of democracy, it is also a matter of aims and objectives. The idea of minimal services for the undeserving poor, with all the implications of a poor standard of provision and contemptuous treatment of applicants dies hard. A welfare system based on the idea of citizenship would mean that everyone would have a right to given opportunities and a given standard of living, and also to a voice in the kind of opportunities and services which were made available.

Thus there are two fundamental requirements for an egalitarian system of welfare : that services should be distributed accordingly to need and that definitions of need should to some extent reflect the wishes of consumers. To what extent is a matter for debate, but the admission of this principle to any degree immediately emphasises the problems of trying to introduce a welfare system of this kind into a society which in other vital respects is very unequal. It is highly unlikely that definitions of their own needs by the poor, in so far as they reflected egalitarian ideologies, would be acceptable to the rich; the result, however, would have to be either some modification of differences in income and opportunities, or conflict, or the abandonment of the citizenship principle.

If welfare services are to be related to need two things follow : need has to be defined and measured in a way which is uniform throughout the country, and services have to be examined and evaluated to see how far they meet that need. As we have already seen, the attempts which local authorities make to define and measure need are very limited; the conception of what constitutes need and the policies devised to meet it vary from one authority to another with the changing political colour of local councils, the changing opinion and power of local officials and the changing need and resources of local populations.

The question of defining need for welfare is especially difficult. Medical needs are defined in relation to the possibilities of cure or treatment, which are determined by the state of medical knowledge. Educational needs are defined in relation to minimum standards of literacy and numeracy and current educational theories, and the service works within a framework of compulsion – parents are required to see that their children have a satisfactory minimum education. In welfare the distinction between healthy and pathological conditions is less clear; it is more dependent on the value judgements of the lay observer and less on the scientific pronouncements of the expert.

In so far as criteria on which services should be available are explicitly formulated, different local authorities and different professional workers have different convictions about how need should be met.[30] Only too often, however, the public authorities make no attempt to measure or search out the needs in their areas but limit their activities to dealing more or less adequately with the cases that become known to them, either because people themselves ask for help or because they are referred by some other agency or person. It is well known that in the past local authorities have made little effort, for instance, to assess need among old people or the handicapped or the mentally ill. Moreover, although more attention has been paid to identifying children or even families in difficulties, the professional social workers concerned with all these groups have largely depended on other officers in the public services and other professional workers – teachers or doctors or nurses – to tell them about people in trouble. Such a referral system is a very uncertain means of discovery, as is demonstrated by the great variations in the proportions of people in different kinds of difficulty known to local authorities and by the many studies which have revealed poor co-operation between social workers.[31]

The identification of need in the welfare services is further complicated in that a wide range of needs for social-work help are defined by administrators and social workers rather than by the people who experience them. Delinquency, poor standards of child care or household management, unsatisfactory personal relationships and other kinds of behaviour which diverge from the conventional norm may all be regarded by officials as indicating a need for some kind of social-work help. But those who flout or disregard conventional standards may take a quite different view of their situation and may prefer to avoid the attentions of social workers. Even when a family or individual may be anxious for the help of a social-work agency, to ask for it emphasises weakness or dependency and amounts to admitting to a kind of problem which is widely regarded with disapproval. There are powerful deterrents which inhibit requests for some forms of welfare help, either because the need for it is not recognised or because the applicant by his very application defines himself to some degree as a deviant.

Reliable measures of need would have to be based on demographic, economic and social analysis of local populations and would probably require regular and systemative surveys to identify those at risk. This kind of monitoring is essential if local authorities are to have an accurate estimate of the size and nature of the problems they are supposed to be tackling. It is also essential as a basis for forecasts of future needs upon which rational planning of the development of the welfare services depends. Attempts by the local authorities to evaluate their services in terms of either their sufficiency or their quality are conspicuously lacking. The studies that have been made have been initiated usually by independent bodies who are especially interested in the welfare of particular groups, or by academics who have a special interest in social policy, or, more recently, by a number of voluntary organisations and pressure groups which have sprung up to advance their various good causes, such as the Child Poverty Action Group or Shelter. If needs are to be attended to efficiently and economically, not only must there be enquiries to establish whether the quantity and quality of services are adequate and satisfactory but there must also be experiments with alternative kinds of provision to test the relative effectiveness and cost of different types of care.

The provision of welfare services on citizenship principles would presumably imply that standards of care supplied by the public authorities would resemble the standard the average person would expect or hope to be able to provide for himself.[32] This concept seems to offer a means of assessing some kinds of welfare services – domestic-help and meals services and opportunities for social activities, for instance – which may be judged according to how far they reach the level which people would choose for themselves given an average income and assuming no handicaps of age or disability. Statements about the need for domiciliary help with domestic work, shopping, preparing meals or for opportunities for meeting other people would depend partly on conventionally accepted ideas about desirable standards of cleanliness, nutrition and social activity and partly on the wishes and inclinations of individuals. Need in relation to institutional accommodation would similarly be defined partly in terms of the conditions preferred and obtained by those able to make their own choices, partly in relation to the wishes of the residents in the homes. Thus judgements about need would take into account the general desire for privacy, for freedom to determine one's own activities (within the limits imposed by age or handicap), to retain personal belongings and for care by considerate and experienced staff who understood the problems of old and handicapped people and sympathised with the special preferences, wishes and idiosyncrasies of particular individuals.

The problems of evaluating the casework elements in the social worker's activities are even more formidable. As has already been suggested there are no established ways of measuring the quality or effectiveness of the counselling, advice and moral support which are an important part of the social worker's job. The complexity of the situations with which social workers have to deal and the consequent difficulty of finding enough similar cases to test different social-work methods and techniques inevitably limit the possibilities of assessment based on valid statistical processes. Furthermore the effectiveness of work with children or families can only be judged by longitudinal studies which continue over many years. What criteria could in any case be used to measure success, and how certainly could results be attributed to the activities of social workers?

The desirability of research which will provide more reliable estimates of the size of problems and allow more realistic planning to meet them is increasingly recognised. The central department has urged local authorities to consider the needs of their areas in planning the development of their domiciliary services[33] and the Seebohm Committee emphasised the vital importance of research as a basis for effective services : 'The planning of the personal social services cannot be undertaken successfully without the research which identifies emerging trends, assesses long-term repercussions, and estimates the character and dimension of future needs.'[34] How effectively local authorities will in fact develop these functions remains to be seen. The Local Authority Social Services Act, 1970, conferred no new powers or duties for research but referred powers already existing under earlier legislation to the new social-services committees. The Chronically Sick and Disabled Persons Act of the same year, however, took a firmer line in making it a duty of local authorities to identify persons who might be eligible for welfare services, to publish information about the services available and to inform people using the services of any others that might be appropriate for them. Once satisfied of the need for certain listed services it became the duty of the local authority to provide them.

Another neglected aspect of the research activities of local authorities is evaluating standards of provision. Again the Seebohm Committee emphasised its importance.

> We urgently need to establish the usefulness of different methods of treating people in obvious need and the effects upon individuals, families and communities of different forms of care. For example, we ought to know far more about the effects upon the families of the mentally subnormal of different kinds of care in the community, or in hospitals. Similarly the advantages and disadvantages of boarding out as opposed to residential care for particular categories of children in care should be carefully assessed. In particular we need a better basis for making choices between alternatives when the decision, once made, may be irreversible and have far-reaching consequences for human happiness.[35]

Evaluative work of this kind hardly exists, though Professor Parker has made a valuable pioneering attempt to show how past experience could be used to guide present practice in placing children in foster homes,[36] and Miss Goldberg has more recently conducted an experiment to try to compare services given to old people by qualified and unqualified workers.[37] Although the conclusions of this latter enquiry are not convincing it is useful as an attempt to establish criteria for judging social work which can be used to assess the activities of different officers, though work with old people is for various reasons easier to evaluate than work with other groups.

There have, of course, been a number of different attempts to improve the quality of local welfare services for particular groups within the framework of the existing distribution of resources. At the end of the 1940s, with the Children's Act promising a better service for children taken into public care, concern arose about children who might be neglected in their own homes, but at that time the solution to the problem was seen to lie in better co-ordination of existing services and better co-operation between existing workers. In the late 1950s the Younghusband Committee looked into the staffing of the local health and welfare departments and emphasised different training arrangements as a way of bringing about better services for the old, the handicapped and the mentally ill. A few years later the Ingleby Committee[38] proposed that local authorities should have extra powers and duties with respect to families in trouble where children might be at risk, and their proposals were accepted and turned into legislation. Meanwhile pressure had been growing since the late 1950s for a structural reorganisation of local-authority departments in the interests of a more accessible, unified and co-ordinated service which would provide more comprehensive and effective care to people in difficulties.[39] The Seebohm Committee supported this approach and made specific recommendations for changing the departmental responsibilities of local authorities which resulted in the Local Authority Social Services Act of 1970.

Concern about the sensitivity of services to needs is linked with the problem of assessing standards of provision; and it also arises out of commitment to the ideal of democratic government. Again, some steps have been taken in the direction of making local services more appropriate and responsive to the needs and wishes of local people. The training of workers, attempts to bring about better co-ordination and co-operation, altering departmental responsibilities and the granting of new powers and duties can all help to refine the services offered. But all these measures work on the supply side, and there is plenty of evidence that such strategies, though necessary, are by no means sufficient. They do not ensure services which are either comprehensible or acceptable to local populations. This would require, first, that local councils should be ready to consult the interests and preferences of the people for whom they are planning and, second, that local officials should be aware of and sensitive to the impression they make on people whom it is their job to help. The preoccupation of some case workers with psycho-analytical techniques, for example, may mean that the assistance they offer appears irrelevant to people who are looking for help with practical or material difficulties.[40]

A more fundamental problem, however, is the question of how welfare services, particularly where financial grants may be involved, can be freed from the taint of charity and poor relief. Mayer and Timms stress the deep-rooted aversion of most of the people in their study to applying for help from the Family Welfare Association, an aversion often coupled with ignorance or mistaken preconceptions about the sort of treatment they might receive. There is little doubt that for many people a request for welfare help amounts to an admission of failure which is felt as deeply humiliating. The relationship with the social worker or welfare officer is an extremely unequal one. Applicants for welfare help are not employing a professional to deal with or advise them about some aspect of their affairs. They are appealing for assistance which may or may not be granted in accordance with rules and procedures which they do not understand, which may be offered in a form quite different from that which they anticipated and which may involve enquiries into the most intimate and personal aspects of their lives. In addition there is the feeling that the very need for public support indicates a loss of independence, a failure to observe customary standards which can only attract public disapproval or, at best, pity. To this extent the notion of citizenship has very little impact on and very little meaning for the mass of applicants for welfare services.[41]

It seems then that local political institutions fail to guarantee that the interests of consumers are either represented in local policy-making or reflected in the quality of local services – understandably enough, as recipients of social-work services tend to be the poorer, less articulate, less educated and less powerful members of their communities. This problem of citizenship rights and democracy in relation to social policy generally has received increasing attention over the past few years. It has led to the welfare-rights movement, which aims to publicise benefits available and encourage people to claim them, involving in some cases a direct challenge to established bureaucratic practices. It has also led to studies of the extent of discussion between local officials and local populations in different areas of planning, and to pressure for more facilities for consultation and stronger local consumer associations so that popular views may be more effectively expressed. Finally it has led to attempts to involve local people not only in planning but also in provision, in the belief that this will lead to better services which will be more effectively used.

The most interesting experiments along these lines are the Education Priority Area and Community Development Project programmes. Fundamental to both is the aim of bringing local inhabitants into active partnership with local officials, social workers or teachers in providing local services. Both programmes have been based on comprehensive surveys of the social and economic character of the local populations, and both have assumed that they must take great care to publicise and explain their objectives and methods to local people and persuade and encourage them to take part in the proposed activities. The debate about community participation in planning and in the supply of services involves separate considerations. It is a debate which raises afresh the old issue of the place of voluntary effort in the welfare state, and it can only be resolved by defining the special contribution that can be made by laymen as opposed to professionals and by voluntary as opposed to statutory workers. The whole discussion has to be related to the value attached to democracy and community, and to conceptions about the proper relationships between individuals and the responsibility which they bear for one another.

NOTES

1. David Owen, *English Philanthropy* (Oxford University Press, 1965) especially parts 2 and 3.
2. See below Chapter 10, pp. 162–5 for further discussion of problems of assessing welfare services.
3. *Social Trends*, no. 1 (1970).
4. Halsey (ed.), *Trends in British Society*, table 12.23.

5. D.H.S.S., *Health and Personal Social Service Statistics for England and Wales* (H.M.S.O., 1972) table 2.9.

6. Ibid. table 1.1.

7. Ibid. table 7.6.

8. Especially among those classified as 'other', that is handicapped persons excluding the blind and the deaf, of whom 86,000 were registered in 1959 compared with 251,000 in 1970. Ibid. table 7.20.

9. Ibid. table 7.15.

10. *Social Trends*, no. 3, table 148.

11. Ibid. table 150.

12. Peter Townsend and Dorothy Wedderburn, *The Aged in the Welfare State* (Bell, 1965); Peter Townsend, *The Last Refuge* (Routledge & Kegan Paul, 1963); Michael Meacher, *Taken for a Ride* (Longman, 1972).

13. Ministry of Pensions and National Insurance, *Financial and Other Circumstances of Retirement Pensioners* (H.M.S.O., 1966) p. 69.

14. Ibid. p. 71, tables V.7 and V.8.

15. Townsend and Wedderburn, *The Aged in the Welfare State*, p. 45.

16. Bleddyn Davies *et al.*, *Variations in Services for the Aged* (Bell, 1971). See also Noel Boaden, *Urban Policy Making* (Cambridge University Press, 1971) for an attempt to identify the factors influencing local policy-making.

17. Amelia I. Harris, *Social Welfare for the Elderly*, vol. 1, Government Social Survey (H.M.S.O., 1968) p. 2.

18. Ibid.

19. Audrey Hunt, *The Home Help Service in England and Wales*, Government Social Survey (H.M.S.O., 1967) pp. 15, 16.

20. Ibid. p. 21.

21. Ibid. p. 25.

22. Sally Sainsbury, *Registered as Disabled* (Bell, 1970). The survey is on a very small scale involving interviews with 211 persons whose names were drawn from the registers of the disabled in London, Essex and Middlesex.

23. Amelia I. Harris, *Handicapped and Impaired in Great Britain*, Office of Population Censuses and Surveys (H.M.S.O., 1971).

24. Ministry of Housing and Local Government, *Staffing of Local Government* (H.M.S.O., 1967).

25. Greta Sumner and Randall Smith, *Planning Local Authority Services for the Elderly* (Allen & Unwin, 1969) section 2.

26. Halsey (ed.), *Trends in British Society*, table 12.7; D.H.S.S., *Health and Personal Social Service Statistics*, table 7.15.

27. Jean Packman, *Child Care: Needs and Numbers* (Allen & Unwin, 1968); Bleddyn Davies, *Social Needs and Resources*.

28. Bleddyn Davies, *Variations in Children's Services among British Urban Authorities* (Bell, 1972).

29. *Report of the Committee on Social Workers in Local Authority Health and Welfare Services* (H.M.S.O., 1959).

30. See Harris, *Social Welfare for the Elderly*; Packman, *Child Care* : *Needs and Numbers*, chap. 13.

31. See, for instance, Barbara N. Rodgers and Julia Dixon, *Portrait of Social Work* (Oxford University Press, 1960); Margot Jefferys, *An Anatomy of the Social Services* (Michael Joseph, 1965); Julia Parker and Rosalind Allen, 'Social Workers in Local Government', *Social and Economic Administration*, vol. 3, no. 1 (January 1969).

32. See below, Chapter 10, p. 162, for further discussion of ways of measuring the adequacy of welfare services.

33. Ministry of Health, *Health and Welfare* : *The Development of Community Care*, Cmnd. 3022 (H.M.S.O., 1966) para. 52.

34. *Report of the Committee on Local Authority and Allied Personal Social Services* (Seebohm Report), Cmnd. 3703 (H.M.S.O., 1968) para. 457.

35. Ibid. para. 463.

36. R. A. Parker, *Decision in Child Care* (Allen & Unwin, 1966).

37. E. Matilda Goldberg, *Helping the Aged* (Allen & Unwin, 1970).

38. Home Office, *Report of the Committee on Children and Young Persons*, Cmnd. 1191 (H.M.S.O., 1960).

39. See Julia Parker, *Local Health and Welfare Services* (Allen & Unwin, 1965) chap. 3, for a discussion of the different proposals to improve local services for children.

40. See John E. Mayer and Noel Timms, *The Client Speaks* (Routledge & Kegan Paul, 1970).

41. See A. M. Rees, 'Access to the Personal Health and Welfare Services', *Social and Economic Administration*, vol. 6. no. 1 (January 1972).

PART III

The Development of Social Policy

CHAPTER 9

Citizenship

Discussions of social policy necessarily raise questions about the values and ideologies which lie behind particular systems; and there are always implications for legislation and administration if a particular set of beliefs about individual rights or collective responsibilities is to be expressed in the public services.

In looking at the welfare needs associated with industrial societies, and the varying response which may be made to them, I have analysed public policies in terms of the degree to which they assume that individual living standards can or should be determined by individual earning power or the possession of wealth rather than by some conception of citizenship rights which are independent of economic position. I now turn to examine the idea of the social rights of citizenship more closely, to see how citizenship would affect the relationship between individuals and public authorities and the policies and procedures which those authorities should pursue.

To argue for a distribution of services or resources based on citizenship principles is to assert that individual living standards should be safeguarded by political decisions which guarantee an agreed level of medical or social care, education, cash, and so on, irrespective of individual bargaining power. Everyone would have the right to share whatever was provided on equal terms with everyone else, similar needs receiving similar treatment with no discrimination in favour of or against particular social, economic, political or racial groups. The idea of citizenship implies that there should be no stigma attached to the use of public services, either because of popular attitudes condemning dependency or as a result of deterrent administrative procedures or poor standards of provision. The quality of the public services would be the best possible, given alternative claims on public resources.

To define the meaning to be attached to citizenship is a relatively easy matter. How far and in what circumstances the idea will ever be widely accepted as a legitimate concept for establishing rights and regulating social relationships is another question. It is obvious that although the idea of citizenship may be claimed as a proper basis for the distribution of a range of public services, yet such a system of distribution and the values it implies are in conflict with many of the practices of a market economy and the ideologies which are associated with and support it. In fact in industrial societies individual living standards are largely determined by economic power or, more precisely, by a man's relation to the labour and capital market. The various jobs and occupations offer different rewards which reflect market forces rather than political decisions about needs.

The clash of interests and values is evident. Market forces and established differentials in wages and salaries give different occupational groups more or less power to determine future wages and working conditions. Moreover, the growing strength of both professions and unions also puts different groups of professionals, managers and workers in more or less powerful positions to influence the political and administrative decisions which tend to determine the distribution of income and welfare in an economy increasingly managed by the state. As to values, on the one hand, hard work, enterprise, independence and wealth are regarded as virtues and measures of success. They enable their possessors to claim goods and services on terms of equality or superiority, they carry prestige and they command respect. On the other hand the notion of citizenship postulates that similar respect be accorded to those who are dependent and poor. That they may have nothing to offer in exchange for the services they receive, except perhaps gratitude, should not damage their self-respect or place them in a position of social inferiority, because the fact of being born into, or recognised as members of, a particular society itself brings entitlement to a defined standard of living and range of opportunities and implies a corresponding range of obligations for other members of that society. The contradiction is clear. Independence, wealth and the ability to buy services of all kinds are highly regarded, but a belief in the idea of citizenship would require their opposites to be similarly approved.

The problem revolves around the notion of reciprocity. Professor Pinker has argued that in any system of exchange self-respect and the respect of others is maintained by the ability to make some return for what is received.[1] Where services are not reciprocated, or where the return or contribution is not clearly linked to the benefit or service, the recipient is stigmatised and the services themselves are likely to be of poor quality and neglected by the public authorities.

Thus in a market system equality in social relationships is maintained by exchanging services for cash, and within the family network by elaborate arrangements for mutual aid. No doubt the uncertainty about family responsibilities for old people and the unwillingness of old people to claim financial and other forms of support from their children, which is very evident in the United States and the rich European countries, reflects the declining contribution which the older generation can make to the material and cultural welfare of the younger in rapidly changing industrial societies. The reciprocal balance of the relationship changes, and the claims of old people become less securely based on the services they give or the authority they wield.

In contrast with exchanges regulated by money or kinship ties, the relationship between givers and receivers of social services has a flimsy reciprocal basis. Applicants for welfare benefit cannot usually support their claim either by cash or by appealing to family loyalties or obligations, and the notion of citizenship is invoked as a substitute. There is no doubt that the values that such a notion implies have a very limited appeal; the idea of citizenship is not effective in preserving a sense of equality and status for the receivers of many state grants, either among the dependants themselves or in the eyes of the rest of the population.

Pinker has argued that stigma – the denial of citizenship – attaches most firmly to those states of dependency which are most complete and prolonged, such as old age and chronic mental or physical incapacity, precisely because the possibilities of services being reciprocated are so remote, and has suggested that this may help to explain the poor quality of public care for these particular groups. The hypothesis is difficult to prove; it also seems likely that the inherent nature of severe mental or physical handicap may inhibit or deter the concern or attention both of the medical profession, who can expect little improvement in the condition of their patients, and of social workers, who may also find their attempts to help unrewarding. From the public at large the chronically disabled tend to be hidden away but, so far as they are visible, they often fail to arouse sympathy. Even if Pinker's hypothesis were correct as a matter of empirical fact, however, that is not to say that such a situation is unchangeable. The problem becomes one of how the attitudes and values which operate to deny citizen status to dependants can be modified and altered.

Nor is it clear how far public opinion requires the receipt of benefits to be legitimised by identifiable contributions or services from the receiver. There is some evidence that insurance payments towards which individuals have contributed are more readily claimed and more widely regarded as respectable than grants made only on test of need by the public-assistance authorities. But whether the explanation lies in the fact that such benefits are linked to individual contributions or that they are distributed without a means test is arguable. It may also be true that war pensions and industrial-injury pensions, linked as they are to some obvious service, are more acceptable than the ordinary old-age pension, but this is largely a matter of speculation at the present time.

Perhaps the stigma attaches not so much to receiving services without making any obvious return, but to the fact that the services offered are often conditional and unpredictable. This is a characteristic which can be used to distinguish different types of social provision. On the one hand there is assistance, such as insurance benefit, available to a defined population in certain circumstances without further enquiry and where conditions of eligibility are clearly laid down according to comprehensible rules. On the other hand is a very different kind of discretionary assistance offered by many of the health, welfare and casework services and by the Supplementary Benefits Commission; here efforts to establish individual needs may involve close enquiry into many aspects of the applicant's personal affairs and relationships, the assistance offered is often a matter of professional discretion, and the principles on which decisions are made may be incomprehensible or unacceptable to the layman. In these circumstances the applicant is not in the situation of demanding a service in return for payment or to which he is entitled through old age, sickness or unemployment and the nature of which he himself can either predict or control. He is, on the contrary, asking for help whose nature and extent is determined by enquiry into and analysis of his needs made by somebody else. In this sense the applicant submits to the decision of the expert and surrenders his claim to equality of status; and feelings of inferiority may be intensified in so far as the treatment or assistance offered by the public authorities, and the attitudes of public officials, reflect society's disapproval of the circumstances which led to the request being made.

It is true, of course, that laymen may defer to professional opinion on matters of which they are ignorant without experiencing any loss of prestige or sense of inferiority, as happens in the National Health Service. The areas over which doctors claim expert skill and knowledge, however, are more clearly limited than those in which social workers operate; nor are judgements about states of health weighted with moral approval or disapproval in the same way as judgements about a person's capacity to manage his personal relationships and economic affairs. The patient moreover retains the important and acknowledged right to choose his doctor and to change him if he is dissatisfied with the attention he receives. In this way he keeps some degree of control over the service offered to him even though he may not be able to judge the quality of the professional care he is given. It is, however, very rarely that the recipient of welfare services has the opportunity to exercise similar rights. Perhaps the different atmosphere surrounding the medical and social-work professions can be related to their different historical origins, traditions and assumptions. Medical science has developed out of efforts to relieve and prevent pain and disability, but a very significant element in social work has been the control of the unruly and degraded poor and their education into what is assumed to be a better way of life. It is difficult both for the practitioners and objects of social work to free themselves entirely of such assumptions and adopt instead the belief in equality of status and esteem that is implied in the idea of citizenship.

The notion of citizenship is linked to other issues which are matters of controversy within social policy; in particular to the debate over selective or universal services and to the question of democratic control and consumer participation in planning and administration.

Selectivity and universality, which form the first major issue, are often presented as opposing principles on which social policies may be based, and the controversy over the merits and acceptability of the two doctrines has intensified over the past few years. But although the supporters of each are firmly entrenched on their opposing sides, nevertheless there remains a great deal of confusion about what the terms actually mean and in practice they may not be so completely in conflict as is often assumed. In fact the universalist approach accepts that some degree of selectivity may be necessary and desirable, and similarly selectivists would agree that some services should follow universal principles. It is the criteria on which selection is made which are at issue and which form the true matter for argument.

How are the two terms to be defined in relation to social policy? Universalism is a feature of those services which are provided without reference to the individual situation of the person receiving them, except in so far as he belongs to the group for which the service is intended. The group may be the whole population : the National Health Service, for instance, covers all people in England and Wales ; or it may be made up of persons of a particular age : all children are entitled to free primary and secondary education; or it may be determined by family situation : family allowances are payable in respect of all dependant children except the first. The insurance scheme is generally considered to be a universal service, but it presents rather special features in that the conditions of eligibility are unusually complicated. Those who benefit must belong to a particular group, such as the old, the sick or the unemployed, but they must also have made a specified number of weekly contributions to the scheme or be the legal dependants of such persons. Furthermore, some benefits last only for a limited time and some are adjusted to individual earnings. The element of universality in any given scheme decreases in so far as the group is defined in a way which excludes others in like circumstances. All sick people may use the National Health Service but only those unemployed men who have paid their contributions may draw unemployment benefit, and what is more their grants will vary not only with their needs, such as the number of their dependants, but with their previous earnings.

No scheme entirely denies the selective principle. Patients receive treatment under the National Health Service according to their medical condition, but no other circumstances, such as occupation or income, are relevant to eligibility though they may influence the actual use made of the service. Perhaps the higher degree of universality in the Health Service to some extent reflects the fact that the need for medical treatment is easier to define objectively than the need for income. Decisions about medicine are in the hands of an established profession, working usually in accordance with widely agreed criteria, whose judgements are in general accepted by laymen. There is no profession in a similar authoritative position to assess income needs, and indeed the whole question of the income a man should receive is entangled in moral arguments which medical care largely escapes. The patient does not have to show that he deserves his treatment, but to gain anything above a minimum subsistence income a man must show a record of some kind of contribution to the economy. Those who for one reason or another have not made any contribution receive only a minimal allowance.

Even if moral character were not at issue there is room for argument about how income needs can be objectively determined and which experts are involved. The present insurance scheme seems to accept that the need for income is a matter partly of subjective feeling and expectation, of customary levels of spending which depend on previous income; it acknowledges the claim of the higher paid to higher allowances when they are out of work. Thus the citizenship principle is limited in the insurance scheme in so far as rights are dependent on contributions which are linked to the ability to earn rather than on judgements about need, and reflect the standard of living a man can win for himself within the market situation rather than his status as a citizen.

Although the conditional element in the insurance scheme limits its universal character, such schemes are quite distinct from those where services depend on means tests. It is the latter kind of discrimination, where resources rather than needs determine eligibility, which has come to be identified with the selectivist approach. Selectivity of this type takes many forms and the tests of means used are very various,[2] but the crucial point is that services or welfare benefits or cash grants depend on the capacity to demonstrate that personal or family income falls below a defined minimum. If this can be shown, and many different minima are used by different agencies as criteria of eligibility for different benefits, then services may be provided free or at reduced charges. The significance of such an arrangement is that rights depend on declaring and establishing some degree of financial poverty, the situation widely viewed within capitalist societies with suspicion, disapproval and hostility.

The universalist/selectivist argument can thus be understood as a controversy about the proper criteria for selection. The universalists, and to this extent they observe citizenship principles, maintain that services should be related to need rather than to individual income. Health and education services should therefore be distributed according to medical condition or intellectual capacity rather than according to ability to pay or social class. And here a conflict of values emerges : a system of universal services tends to restrict the choices of individuals. Services would be distributed on the principle that similar needs should receive similar attention; the possibility that individuals might, in defining their own needs and given that they had the resources, arrange for themselves a different kind of provision from that received by others in a like situation would conflict with the universalist approach. The essence of the universal type of service is that everyone is treated impartially; none can command a higher quality of provision or claim a larger share of national resources because of social, economic or political power.

Sometimes, however, the universalist approach has meant not so much treating similar cases in a similar way but treating different cases in a similar way in order to avoid distinguishing a group which could be labelled as inferior. Beveridge's social-insurance scheme required similar contributions and offered similar benefits to people with widely different incomes and needs. The refusal to discriminate according to income and the insistence that everyone should 'stand in on the same terms' was considered by Beveridge to be a most important feature of the scheme and it may be seen as one expression of universalist principles. Equality of treatment was an indication of the equal respect and status accorded to everyone. By contrast public assistance was and is dependent on a means test and the amount of cash granted varies with the applicant's resources. This particular type of selectivity, which requires an admission of financial poverty, is perhaps the one which provokes the strongest feelings; a reflection of prevailing opinion which finds economic dependence reprehensible to a greater degree than sickness, homelessness or unemployment, for instance.

To distribute benefits in accordance with financial need thus has the consequence of defining a group of persons who tend to be stigmatised as inferior. The principle of services according to need which, it has been argued, lies behind the universal services has a different meaning in the context of income because the need in question is itself regarded as a mark of failure. It is this label that universal services where benefits are available without reference to income avoid. The other critieria of selection which may be used do not carry the same implications of social rejection. On the contrary they emphasise the similarity in the status of those who receive the services; they imply no kind of moral distinction between those who can and those who cannot support themselves. Indeed, Professor Marshall goes further and sees the universal social services as positively encouraging social equality and so reducing the significance of economic inequality.

That citizenship principles imply universal services does not mean that selective policies necessarily deny such principles. On the contrary, the idea of positive discrimination, recently introduced into social policy, can be an indispensable means to the realisation of citizen rights. This follows when the definition of equality is broadened to include the assertion that social policies, if they are to aim at equality, must not only guarantee similar educational opportunities, for example, but also similar chances to use those opportunities. Such objectives inevitably lead to selectivity; given that a child's family background and material circumstances greatly influence his performance in school, children from poor homes can only be given an equal chance to learn if measures are taken to compensate for the educational handicaps imposed by their environment : hence the arguments in the Plowden Report for a con-centration of resources and effort in educational priority areas – both to raise the quality of the education offered and to stimulate and encourage parental and community interest in it. Similar treatment for all children was explicitly rejected in favour of discriminatory services to give priority to the greatest need.

It is important to recognise the special nature of such discriminatory policies and to distinguish them from other types of selectivity which do in fact deny the rights of citizenship. Many services based on selection have a very deterrent flavour. In some cases the means test acts as a device for limiting the claims on public funds and where those claims have to be acknowledged the help given is very meagre – as with cash grants from the Supplementary Benefits Commission. The initiative for claiming services or grants also lies with the individual rather than the public authority; a man must apply for supplementary benefit or a rent allowance or a uniform grant for his children.

Positive discrimination, on the other hand, as the idea has been developed within education, distinguishes people for unusually favour-able treatment in order to try to compensate for disadvantages inherent in their physical environment or upbringing. Moreover, the onus is on the public authorities to identify and search out those groups in special need and to encourage and teach them to make full use of whatever services are available for them. The test of need is not one which requires proof of economic poverty, though many of the inhabitants of educational priority areas are indeed poor. Nor is the assistance given calculated in terms of what is necessary to reach a defined minimum standard of living, but is determined instead by theories about the most effective ways of helping people to make the most of their opportunities and experience.

The second major issue which is linked to the citizenship principle is the matter of democratic control and consumer participation in the planning and administration of social policy. There are two questions involved. One concerns the weight to be given to the opinions and preferences of laymen and consumers, as opposed to those of officials and professionals, in the planning and execution of policy. The other is the way in which applicants for welfare benefits are treated by the personnel in welfare departments.

The extent to which laymen and consumers should share in policy-making and administration is a question which has attracted increasing attention over the past few years. The meaning of the citizenship principle in this context is fairly plain. The kind of equality of status implied in the idea of citizenship carries with it the right to take part in the planning of services which vitally affect people's lives and in decisions which do not call for some kind of professional or expert knowledge not possessed by the layman. Similarly, it carries the right of enquiry into and criticism of customary forms of provision or administrative procedures.

The crucial problem here is to distinguish those kinds of decision which should be left to the professionals or officials because they depend on a body of skill, experience or specialised knowledge which the layman or ordinary consumer does not have, and those in which the consumer should take part because he is the only 'expert' available. Or to put it another way, it is a problem of deciding how far and in what circumstances the professional's claim to know best what is good for other people may be justified.

Recent developments in social policy show increasing awareness of and concern about this issue. The American 'war on poverty' and the insistence (written into the legislation) on the participation of the poor in developing programmes to assist them – a policy whose problems have been effectively demonstrated both by academic criticism and by experience[3] – was a recognition of the claims of the poor to have some say in determining their own destinies as far as welfare arrangements were concerned. Similarly one aim of the community-development projects in this country, both governmental and voluntary, is to encourage local people to articulate and express their views, and to see that popular wishes and preferences are actively brought to bear on and taken into account in decision-making. This concern to encourage local participation is both reflected in and perhaps strengthened by a variety of official enquiries and reports.[4]

In the debate about the significance to be attached to bureaucratic opinion on the one hand and consumer preferences on the other, some matters seem to be generally accepted as suitable for decision by experts – in particular those services, such as medicine, which are dispensed by professionals employing knowledge and techniques beyond the grasp of the layman who does not have the necessary training. In medicine, doctors have established their ability to treat successfully a fairly wide range of illnesses, and their right to take decisions about appropriate treatment for particular cases goes largely unchallenged;[5] it is assumed that the doctor, by virtue of his professional knowledge, will be better able to make decisions about the kind of medical care that is needed than the patient.

In other services, measures of the success of particular methods, or the rightness of particular decisions which are independent of the patient or consumer, are less easy to obtain, and the claims of the administrators to take decisions on the basis of some kind of expert knowledge are more suspect. The distinction is between those services based on a substantial body of knowledge and experience, where the efficacy of given methods in achieving particular ends has been established through a long period of experiment, and those where professional knowledge and skill is lacking or undeveloped, where the relation of means to ends is much less certain, or where the ends themselves may be in question. Planning decisions fall into this latter group. Beyond a certain point, where housing is so bad as to threaten health, decisions about demolition and redevelopment increasingly become a matter for general debate. There are no established professional principles which clearly indicate the right course of action. Planning decisions often involve an appeal to aesthetic standards, which may themselves be controversial and not susceptible to any kind of expert adjudication. Or the relevance of such considerations, as opposed to the preferences of the people whose houses are to be knocked down, may be denied. Similarly, there are many welfare services where need must, to some degree, be defined by the individual concerned. In so far as services have as their object the enhancement of individual well-being, then judgements about their desirability or effectiveness must depend to a large extent on the satisfaction of those who receive them.

The second aspect of democratic control and consumer participation in social policy, the treatment of applicants for welfare benefits, has also become something of a public issue over the past few years. One essential element in the idea of citizenship is that it involves a range of rights which derive from that status and not from any other characteristics, for example economic position or family background, of the person in question. Thus, if citizenship were invoked as a principle which should inform the social services, it would mean that applicants for welfare benefits should receive the same kind of consideration and respect as would be accorded to anyone making his own private arrangements for similar services. Over the past ten or twenty years, awareness of such rights has begun to penetrate the administration, particularly perhaps in hospitals and in the Supplementary Benefits Commission, but much remains to be done before it is fully realised.

Nor is it simply a matter of treating applicants with superficial courtesy; it is, perhaps, more important that they should receive comprehensible and adequate information about the full extent of their rights to claim particular benefits and to appeal against adverse decisions by the authorities.[6] Such rights may remain relatively empty and meaningless if the inexpert layman has to challenge the accumulated knowledge and experience of the administration. Professional advice and guidance should be available to anyone entering into dispute with a public authority to enable him to present his case as effectively as possible.

An attempt to provide services of a high standard which were responsive to the wishes of the people who used them, would also have clear implications for the organisation and staffing of welfare departments. In some ways social-service agencies conform to the classical model of a bureaucratic organisation. They are hierarchical. Their staff have specialised functions, work according to an elaborate set of regulations, and are full-time salaried employees who depend on the organisation for their livelihood. Social-service departments share with other bureaucracies a tendency to rigidity, to conservatism, and an anxiety to preserve their own power;[7] and the working-to-rule, which is partly an attempt to ensure similar treatment for similar cases, can lead to the neglect of special needs. Furthermore, dependence on the organisation for a job may mean that employees hesitate to criticise the established policies of their departments even if they believe those policies to be working against the rights or the welfare of the people they are supposed to serve. In many branches of the social services, bureaucratic characteristics are modified in so far as employees are professionals who claim some discretion in interpreting their duties and responsibilities in the light of the skill and knowledge they have gained through their training. Professional social workers are taught to observe loyalties to the people they are trying to help as well as to the organisation that employs them. Nevertheless some officers display attitudes which are a denial of rights or of respect, and this will only change with more widespread training, more careful selection and deliberate attempts to inculcate different values.

Sympathy and respect for the poor are not, in any case, enough, and they may be dangerous. It is easy and quite common for social workers to combine both these attitudes with the assumption that poverty or social breakdown, whatever form it takes, is either inevitable or an expression of personal maladjustment which is properly treated by casework methods. This kind of approach can be fatal for fundamental reforms. If the social services are to be used to discover social needs and to define social problems, which would be a vital function if social policies were based on citizenship principles, social workers must be constantly aware of poverty as an expression of the social structure and the social distribution of rewards and opportunities. The essential question then becomes not how to support those who suffer it, though this of course is a necessary and important activity, but how to change the institutions of society to stop it happening.

This brings us back to the root of the problem. However sympathetic and sensitive the authorities may be to the varieties of human needs, however respectful of human dignity and however meticulous in informing people of their rights, the essential requirements for policies based on citizenship principles are high standards of service and provision that is adequate. So far as Britain is concerned this would require a major re-allocation of resources to the public sector.

Radical reformers usually think in terms of government activity when changing social institutions is at issue. But there are other dimensions to the conception of a good society, which allot public authorities and bureaucracies a much smaller place. Professor Titmuss approaches the matter in a different way; in his last book[8] he was expressing his faith not in the activities of governments but in a particular kind of relationship between the governed as pointing the way to the welfare society. For Titmuss the essential basis of civilised social life lies in the readiness of men and women to accept responsibility for one another, to the point of offering services to strangers, without any hope or expectation of future return. This disinterested benevolence, above all else, is indispensable for a united society; and where it is missing the quality of social relationships inevitably suffers. Thus it becomes important not only to avoid, wherever possible, systems of exchange or supply based on market principles, but also to avoid government activity which might undermine or discourage that kind of voluntary mutual aid and altruism which is expressed in the gift relationship. Viewing social legislation in this light Titmuss acclaims the ideals on which the National Health Service was based but deplores, for instance, the payment of foster parents on the grounds that the introduction of market values damages the quality of the care that is offered. The message is essentially a simple one: unless men feel, and express in their actions, concern and compassion for one another, no amount of government coercion or lavish provision through the market will lead to an integrated and stable society. On the contrary, human relations will be impoverished and society in imminent danger of disintegration. This raises in a new form the old controversy about the place of voluntary effort in a welfare state. It becomes less a question of the part voluntary effort can play within the public services and more a matter of the part that the public services can play in fostering and encouraging voluntary action. This puts our problem of the proper relations between welfare authori ties and officials and the people they serve in a different perspective. Whatever else it may suggest, Titmuss's advocacy lends powerful support to the policies pursued in the educational priority areas and community development projects of encouraging people to take part in both the planning and provision of community activities and services.

NOTES

1. Robert Pinker, *Social Theory and Social Policy* (Heinemann, 1971) chap. 4.

2. See, for instance, Mike Reddin, *Social Services for All? Part One*, Fabian Tract 382 (1968).

3. See, for instance, Moynihan, *Maximum Feasible Misunderstanding*; and *On Fighting Poverty*, ed. Sundquist.

4. See, for instance, *Royal Commission on Local Government in England 1966–1969*, Cmnd. 4040 (H.M.S.O., 1969); Seebohm Report; *People and Planning: Report of the Committee on Public Participation in Planning* (H.M.S.O., 1969); *National Health Service Reorganisation*, Cmnd. 5055 (H.M.S.O., 1972).

5. It is, of course, subject to both economic and moral constraints; very expensive forms of treatment are limited, and patients and their families may refuse treatment recommended for them.

6. It is also important, of course, that those rights should exist! J. C. Kincaid in *Poverty and Equality in Britain* (Penguin, 1973) points to the significant differences in the rights of appeal against decisions on insurance benefits and those taken by officials of the Supplementary Benefits Commission.

7. See Marris and Rein, *Dilemmas of Social Reform*; and Moynihan, *Maximum Feasible Misunderstanding*.

8. R. M. Titmuss, *The Gift Relationship* (Allen & Unwin, 1970).

CHAPTER 10

Policy Implementation

In relation to any activity planning implies establishing ends and deciding on ways of reaching them. If this is to be a rational process, means have to be related to ends in such a way as to ensure the greatest effectiveness and economy – or whichever of these two is preferred – and this in turn implies research. But while all policy-making must involve establishing aims, measuring needs and assessing the efficiency of services, these problems become more urgent when policies attempt to express citizenship values which reject the market as a determinant of living standards, and subsistence as appropriate for dependants, and aim at a distribution of income and services based on a conception of common needs which reflects a belief in individual rights independent of individual income or wealth.

The problem of deciding aims is complicated by the inherent difficulty of formulating a definition of welfare which is sufficiently precise to serve as a viable policy objective, and by conflicts in values which may preclude agreement about what aims should be set or which should be given priority. If the idea of citizenship implies that those who share that status have similar rights to similar standards of medical care, education or welfare irrespective of their power to buy the relevant services, then public provision for dependants would have to be related to the standards that the average member of society would choose for himself. In other words public policy, in so far as it expressed citizenship values, would aim at a level of welfare reflecting normal hopes and expectations rather than at the minimum necessary for survival. Although the exact relationship of the situation of dependants to the rest of the community might be matter for argument, some relationship would have to be established which could be clearly enough defined for it to serve as an objective for planning and administration.

The problems involved in such definitions of aims are relatively manageable in the case of income services. If benefits based on subsistence needs are abandoned, it is simple to relate cash payments to average income per head, in principle, because cash income can be relatively easily measured and cash benefits therefore can be established at whatever proportion of the average it is decided they should represent. Setting standards for welfare, or indeed for health or education, which reflect an agreed relation to the norm or the average is another matter. Public welfare services, institutional and domiciliary, may be seen either as an alternative or a support to independent living or family care. But to define a concept which would reflect the average experience of welfare is difficult because such information about people's personal lives is not available and, even if it were, a notion of welfare would depend on so many different elements – some of them representing the quality rather than the quantity of human experience or relationships – that to construct an idea of an average state which could serve as a guide for public services would be a very complex exercise.

It is not, however, impossible to formulate some sort of model which would take into account the common desire for a given level of economic, material, physical and social well-being. For old people it would mean a guarantee of sufficient income, however defined, adequate medical care and comfortable material living conditions, with opportunities for both privacy and sociability according to the inclinations of the persons concerned. It need hardly be pointed out that policies committed to, and realising, such objectives would revolutionise the British welfare system.

The problems with regard to children are more complicated. Here it is a matter of deciding not only appropriate standards of amenity and comfort for children in public care but also of providing the sort of environment most likely to turn them into capable and socially acceptable adults. In some cases it is a question of determining at what point a family situation becomes so bad as to justify removing a child from his parents' care. Such decisions are bedevilled by uncertainty about the effect on children of particular circumstances and about the psychological damage which may be done by taking a child away from his home, even where there are obvious signs of physical or emotional neglect or deprivation. There is also the difficulty of deciding what weight to give to the wishes of parents who want to keep their children with them even if it can be established that this is against a child's best interests. These dilemmas may reflect conflicts in values but they also arise from the lack of certain knowledge about how circumstances influence a child's development, knowledge hard to achieve when each child's personality introduces further variables into the situation. There are, of course, guiding principles which can be used, such as the desirability for a child of a continuing secure and affectionate relationship with his mother. But this is not in dispute; the difficulties arise where such a relationship does not exist or is badly damaged, or when other circumstances lead to the separation of parent and child, and where it becomes a question of how the situation should be repaired.

The setting of aims for education which would reflect citizenship values is also complicated by lack of knowledge, as well as by conflicts over which aims should have priority. The state educational system in Britain has moved over the past hundred years through several phases.[1] During the first half of this century, universal elementary education was supplemented by limited opportunities for secondary education for particularly clever working-class children, but in 1944 this system gave way to the idea that secondary education should be provided for all. Since the Second World War, however, it has become widely recognised that equal chances to go through some form of secondary schooling in no way produce equal opportunities to profit from it because, even leaving aside the varying quality of secondary education, a child's achievement in his school is heavily influenced by his home situation. Those who wanted equality of opportunity, therefore, began to insist that this would only be realised if some form of compensatory education were introduced for those children who were handicapped by a poor family background. More recently, doubts have arisen as to how far even a perfectly realised meritocratic system properly represents citizenship values. Perhaps the emphasis on providing a traditional academic education for all able children is misplaced? If the social and occupational structure of a country is such that the majority of children are destined for manual and clerical jobs rather than for professional and managerial occupations, and if many of them will inevitably remain in decayed urban environments characterised by the concentration of social problems typical of the E.P.A.s, then a more appropriate objective for education might be to equip those children to understand and tackle the physical, social and economic problems which surround them. The two aims are not necessarily incompatible. The emphasis on a kind of education which is relevant for and linked to a child's immediate environment can also be an attempt to provide a meaningful experience through which he will then more readily develop his abilities.

None the less, this illustration from education shows that aims may be difficult to set, not only because of the problems of defining the desired states of welfare but also because it may be unclear exactly what aims are consistent with citizenship values. Furthermore, aims, or at any rate the possibility of achieving them, are always limited by resources and technical skill. Policy objectives have to be weighed against one another and priorities have to be established in the light of continuing research to explore social conditions and social needs.

Although it is obvious that rational decisions about aims and priorities presuppose accurate knowledge of social conditions, it is also true that any attempt to collect relevant data rests on prior assumptions about the aims in view. Efforts to measure the state of a population's health or delinquency rates are most likely to occur in a situation where the government is already committed to providing health services and controlling crime. The problem of devising reliable social indicators is becoming more obvious as interest in the matter develops. The form of indicator which will be most appropriate depends on the purpose it is intended to serve, and three uses have been distinguished – to reveal social situations, to judge the effectiveness of policy, and to give warning of emerging problems.[2] As we have suggested, indicators have but a limited use in the first sense, in that they will often reveal social conditions only in so far as a particular area of enquiry is already regarded as significant for policy-making. From this it would follow that their use in the third sense, in detecting problems as yet unrecognised, is also limited.

If the use of indicators is examined in the first sense, it is fairly clear that they do not in fact reveal very much about social conditions. Their significance emerges only as the facts they record are related to other knowledge and interpreted in the light of a particular set of values. Statistics about the incidence of particular diseases or, as is more common, about death rates mean little until they are placed in a historical or comparative context, so that changes, in infant-mortality rates for example, can be related to changes in physical environment, incomes, health services, standards of nutrition, and so on.

Furthermore, the attempt to assess complex matters such as standards of health raises difficulties about the weight to be given to different indices. How far does an increase in the incidence of heart disease or cancer cancel out a decrease in tuberculosis? And how can such various independent measures be summed up to produce an overall judgement about the health condition of a population and whether it is changing for better or for worse? What weight is to be given to degrees of pain or of physical or social disability imposed by different illnesses? The problems involved in such composite measures are formidable; but any comprehensive index of health must attempt to measure both intensity and duration of illness and encompass both medical data and social judgements.[3]

Quite apart from the difficulties of devising indicators for complex phenomena, the influence such indicators have on policy formation depends on many other factors than their own reliability; for example, on whether the action which the indicator suggests is costly, on how far it is politically controversial, and on whether it would be administratively complicated to introduce.[4] Social indicators are not in themselves indicators of the directions policy should take. As Shonfield has pointed out, they reveal situations, but deductions about the implications for policy assume value judgement about what changes or what action may be appropriate.

Indicators are also required in the second of the senses distinguished on p. 161 to judge the effectiveness of policies. There is no easy way of knowing how far public provision in fact meets the needs that it aims to supply. The checks that operate in a market situation where dissatisfied customers can choose an alternative product or service do not usually exist in public-welfare services, which tend to be monopolies offering little choice to consumers. It thus becomes all the more important to find an alternative measure of quality. It cannot be assumed that failure to meet needs will necessarily arouse public interest, either among those for whom the services are intended or among those who administer them. In the first place, it is now a familiar fact that large numbers of people who receive public services or benefits are not effective critics of their standards. This may be due to lack of knowledge about what they are entitled to expect, to lack of confidence or education, or it may be because there is no clear and easy way of registering protests or opinions. Such a situation can be remedied to some degree by better publicity, more help for people to express their views, and setting up procedures for considering criticisms.

There is a second reason why the assessment of services should not be left to the people who use them. Often the process of evaluation is so complicated or so dependent on professional knowledge that the layman or consumer may be able to make only a partial judgement. Thus while it may be reasonable in the case of an old people's home, for example, to judge the quality of the institution largely in terms of the old people's satisfaction with their comfort and the attention they receive, it would be less reasonable to judge the standard of a hospital ward in terms of the satisfaction of the patients who, as laymen with limited experience, cannot weigh the medical care they receive, or even the organisation of the ward they inhabit, against alternatives of which they are probably ignorant. Patients will often be unable to judge how far a deterioration or improvement in their own condition reflects the quality of their treatment or the inevitable progress of their disease.[5]

If, therefore, there can be no dependable or complete evaluation of public services by consumers, it follows that some other way of assessing them must be found if citizenship principles are to be observed and services related to needs. The alternative is that the public authorities themselves should take responsibility for evaluation. There are some indications, as we have seen, that this is beginning to happen. But the problems are many and formidable. On the one hand are those problems to which we have already referred – of deciding on suitable criteria of judgement and the weight that should be given to the judgements of professionals, administrators and officials, or of patients and consumers. On the other hand, and at a different level, are the problems surrounding the relations between government and research, between politicans and academics, and the likely conflict in values and priorities which make the two uneasy partners.

Attempts to evaluate services often involve comparisons with other administrative areas or other similar organisations. In practice, high rates of expenditure, the 'extensiveness' or 'intensiveness' of services, high ratios of staff to population, and high proportions of professionally qualified staff are often regarded as indications of high standards.[6] All these measures are hazardous and none can be used in isolation. Moreover, they are all measures of supply, which to be meaningful have to be related to measures of need, and the latter barely exist. High expenditure may reflect high costs rather than high standards, and the implications of high ratios of staff or accommodation to population can only be judged in relation to their quality. This latter point raises a more fundamental difficulty. It is generally assumed that professionally qualified staff can offer better services than untrained personnel, but there are no established criteria for judging the performance of social workers which might be used to verify this assumption.[7] It requires an initial act of faith in the power and skill of professionally trained workers which cannot at present be demonstrated. In a strict sense the measures are circular.

In a similar way, we make assumptions about the desirability of different types of provision, but the evidence to justify our preferences is not clearly established. What, in any case, would count as evidence? The happiness of a child in public care, for instance, or its success in its future career? And how are these to be assessed? Judgements about the desirability of one kind of service rather than another can only be validated by carefully planned research and controlled experiments. The standard which represents adequacy is also very much at issue. How many visits to children in foster homes amount to adequate supervision? How much domestic help is adequate for an old person living alone? What criteria can be used for judging good social work or a good school? These are the crucial questions that have to be answered before reliable assessments of the social services can be made.

Moreover, although assessments should not be left entirely to consumers or laymen, judgements about adequacy would have to take some account of the views of the persons for whom the services were intended. This again is linked to the idea that people as citizens have rights to a given standard of services which it is not an act of benevolence or charity but a duty of the state to supply.[8] In practice, many branches of the social services bear the stamp of ideologies which associate public services with the undeserving poor, for whom minimal standards are thought to be appropriate. The poor quality of care, lack of privacy and undue regimentation in some old people's homes and other institutions, the inconsiderate treatment of applicants for grants in some social-security offices and the failure of many hospitals to introduce proper appointment systems all testify to attitudes which deny rights to equality of treatment and define those receiving public help as socially inferior. Serious concern for equality would mean establishing and publicising procedures within the social services for dealing with complaints and receiving suggestions for improvements. Much more would have to be done to canvass opinion about the kind of services or amenities that people wanted. There would have to be more opportunity for choice between different kinds of institutions or between institutional or domiciliary care, and where appropriate services would be democratically organised.

A more intractable problem, perhaps, arises from the inevitable conflicts between policy-makers and researchers, which can never be completely resolved and which require some degree of compromise and sacrifice on both sides if a useful working relationship is to develop.[9] The problem exists because the greater part of social research is dependent upon government funds which are necessarily limited, while the possible objects of research are almost unlimited. Furthermore, the interests of policy-makers and researchers may not coincide, and limited resources require that priorities be established.

In any branch of government policy-makers are, above all, concerned to introduce programmes or activities which they believe will have a significant influence on some defined problem or will be effective in changing a given state of affairs to bring about a particular end. If results are not apparent there will be a temptation to substitute some alternative scheme in the hope of quicker returns; politicians are sensitive to, and to some degree controlled by, public reactions to their policies. Researchers may also be concerned with discovering the most effective way of realising a given end, particularly in the kind of action-research which has been a feature of work in the E.P.A. and Community Development projects. But they are also interested in identifying cause and effect, in assessing the results of particular actions, even though those results may not have been the ones intended or desired by the planners. The researcher is constrained by his discipline, by the need to observe the rules of scientific enquiry, if he wants to maintain the professional standards which will make his conclusions valid. The primary aim of the administrator or politician is to make sure that something happens, to concentrate resources or action on a given problem, but the first ambition of the researcher is to understand why things happen as they do. This may mean, among other things, the selection of control groups, where the consequences of a particular kind of intervention for a particular group are to be assessed, and it certainly means careful and precise measurement or description of situations before and after innovations are introduced. For the planner these activities may seem unnecessarily elaborate given the urgency of the problem to be tackled.

In the case of action-research, which may involve programmes that can only be evaluated over a number of years, there is always the temptation to alter or extend the original programme in the light of new experience. But, if he is to guard the validity of his experiment, the researcher must resist attempts to modify it until he has had the chance to assess it. Even negative results, which for planners and administrators represent failure, are significant for research in ruling out particular hypotheses and encouraging the formulation of new theories.

This concern with the relationship of research and experiment to theory and knowledge rather than to action and change emerges in another sense. It is very common for administrators and planners to reject proposals to investigate the extent of particular problems or needs, on the grounds that those which are already known tax existing services beyond available resources. For officials and politicians who are trying to meet more demands than they have the means to satisfy this is a telling argument. But for researchers, who are not responsible for organising services and who are much less vulnerable to public pressure, it is even more essential to explore the full dimensions of need to reach an accurate understanding of the problems the administration has to tackle. Only in this way will there be an opportunity for rational decisions about priorities based on as much knowledge as may be obtainable about the urgency of different claims on resources.

The relationship between government and research, between policy-makers and researchers, in the social sciences has come sharply into focus in the recent E.P.A. and Community Development programmes. In the first of these the action and research activities were closely bound together, and their significance for one another was discussed and debated by all concerned in the programme before the local projects started, so that guiding objectives and principles were firmly established from the beginning. Even so, differences in priorities and in emphasis remained and are obvious in the final reports from the areas concerned. In some districts researchers and those responsible for the action side of the project worked more harmoniously together than in others; and some projects concentrated on the maximum number of activities while others preferred to limit action in the interests of careful and sophisticated evaluation.

In both the E.P.A. and the Community Development experiments, however, research and action were linked together on an *ad hoc* basis and in the interests of a particular enquiry into a particular problem. If research is to become an integral part of the normal process of policy-making and administration, then new and different problems of organisation emerge. Most important is the inescapable fact that the resources allocated for research on social policy will always be limited and will always fall far short of what would be necessary to follow up all possible or desirable lines of investigation. In such a situation of scarcity there must be some established way of deciding priorities and avoiding overlapping and duplication of work. This raises questions about the responsibility of the central departments concerned with social policy, about the relations of civil servants with academics, and about the relations between central government and local authorities.

At present there are various grant-giving bodies which operate within the general area of social policy, ranging from the interested ministries (particularly the Home Office, the Department of Health and Social Security and the Department of Education and Science), through the statutory research councils to the independent foundations. It is unrealistic to suppose that any substantial measure of control could be exercised over the activities of the Trusts by any statutory governmental agency, but an essential step towards creating a more rational system would be to set up a body to be responsible for the research activities sponsored by the government departments and research councils. Such a body would have as its main function the review of all applications for research funds, first to see that the aims and methods of the proposed enquiries gave fair promise of significant results, second to co-ordinate research activities, to detect any investigations which duplicated one another and to bring together people engaged on related enquiries, and third to recommend priorities among the competitors for awards.

Quite apart from the grants to outside bodies, mainly universities, a certain amount of research is conducted within the ministries concerned with social policy. But the research side of the work of the central departments is in general poorly developed, and there are few officers with social-science qualifications. All the ministries should have the facilities and resources for their own research, with appropriate recruitment policies and career opportunities for professional social researchers. The internal research activities of the departments should, of course, also come under review by the central social-policy research body.

This kind of responsibility, which is centralised in the interests of economy and efficiency and to permit a rational ordering of priorities, has its dangers. Research must never be dominated or determined by immediate problems of politics and administration. The most useful research may well take the form of enquiries or experiments designed to test theories and hypotheses and so to contribute to the formation of a wider body of theoretical knowledge rather than to clarify or alleviate a particular problem.[10] Researchers must retain some freedom to design their investigations in a way they believe will advance the academic study of the social sciences; in other words, the possibility of independent enquiry must be preserved.

Let us now consider the second question. The need to strike a balance between the claims of immediately pressing political problems and those of 'pure' research suggests that any controlling body must be composed of a mixture of academic social scientists, civil servants from the relevant departments, including representatives from the local authorities, and politicians. Moreover, the partnership between academics and civil servants should extend further than common membership of a formal body. Arrangements should be worked out whereby outside researchers could have access to departmental records and statistics, and it should be considered how far departmental practices and methods in collecting and presenting data might be altered to meet the needs of research.[11] Obviously there are limits to any such proposal; some information which administrators require may be of little value to research and in any case the needs of research cannot always be anticipated. But it is desirable that there should be some rationalisation and standardisation of the process of collecting and analysing statistics by both central and local government.

This brings us to the third question – the relations between central departments and local authorities. It is clear enough from the above arguments that the overseeing of research activities of local government, as of the central departments, should be subject to review by the national body responsible for research in all areas of social policy. This is especially important for two reasons. First, the desire of local councils to avoid increasing the burden on local rates might inhibit the development of research activities at a local level, particularly if that research were likely to reveal a need for a great expansion of local services. This could well mean that research should be entirely financed from national funds. Second, and also a further argument for central financing, local councillors are inevitably vulnerable to local opinion, and the removal of the costs of research to central government would protect local politicians from pressure to spend available resources on better services rather than on the less obviously rewarding enquiries into needs which it might not in any case be possible to meet.

Furthermore, research to assess standards of provision or the effectiveness of different ways of organising services would be wastefully duplicated if local authorities were independently carrying out similar enquiries in their own districts. This is not to argue that all initiative in research should pass from the local bodies. On the contrary, the particular and various problems encountered by local authorities might be significant in suggesting new lines of enquiry. The central department would have a co-ordinating and advisory role as well as the responsibility for recommending priorities in the light of the resources available. The advisory role would be particularly important, especially in the early stages when qualified social researchers would be scarce and when some local authorities would have to rely on unqualified and inexperienced people. In this situation a central body which could provide expert advice about research design and techniques would be essential. In the beginning it might well be that a large proportion of the research undertaken locally would be initiated by the central organisation; but as the local teams would be more closely in touch with the immediate problems of their areas and of local administration they could be expected to play an increasing part in putting forward proposals as they became more experienced and more professional.

NOTES

1. See Harold Silver, *Equal Opportunity in Education* (Methuen, 1973) for a collection of documents illustrating the course of the discussion since the 1920s.

2. Elaine Carlisle, 'The Conceptual Structure of Social Indicators', in *Social Indicators and Social Policy*, ed. Shonfield and Shaw.

3. A. J. Culyer, R. J. Lavers and Alan Williams, 'Health Indicators', ibid.

4. Richard Rose, 'The Market for Policy Indicators', ibid.

5. See Keith Hope and Angela Skrimshire, 'Hospital Efficiency', *Social and Economic Administration*, vol. 6, no. 2 (May 1972).

6. See Davies, *Social Needs and Resources*.

7. See Goldberg, *Helping the Aged*, for a rather unsuccessful attempt to explore this problem.

8. See above, Chapter 8, p. 133.

9. Halsey, *Educational Priority*, chap. 13.

10. The problem of the balance between 'useful' and 'pure' research arises acutely in medicine. See Louis Goldman, *When Doctors Disagree* (Hamish Hamilton, 1973).

11. The problems of using official statistics and their frequent inadequacy for research puposes is demonstrated in Halsey (ed.), *Trends in British Society*.

Conclusions

Society is made up of men and women who group themselves into families, communities, industrial organisations, professional associations, trade unions and political parties in order to carry on the business of living, bringing up children, pursuing their occupations and deciding how the fruits of their various labours are to be shared among themselves. The system of production and the nature of the distribution of goods, services, opportunities and rewards are of crucial importance in determining the character of any society, and both are at once a response to and an influence upon other elements in the social structure. The available scientific knowledge and technology, family and kinship organisation, differences of geography, class and race, and prevailing ambitions, beliefs and ideologies all combine to create a complicated pattern of demand and need for a range of activities, experiences, possessions and opportunities. Social policy may be defined as the set of theoretical and working principles in terms of which two broad aspects of society, the supply of and demand for welfare goods and services, are related through public organisation.

This book has been about social policy in this sense. I have tried to relate two aspects of British social structure in describing first the needs and demands for welfare which arise and second the supply of public arrangements which responds to these and contributes to a particular distribution of income, health, education, housing and welfare. The importance of social policy in Britain and other urban-industrial countries is indicated by the vast and growing resources, amounting to a third of the total national output, which it absorbs.

My main object has been to describe the social services in terms of social demand and public supply. Descriptions, however, usually imply explanations; and it is desirable to make the implications explicit. In conclusion, therefore, I want to discuss the explanation of social policy and to specify what I take to be the explanatory implications of the descriptions I have offered.

Part 1 contains a sketch of three models for social policy – *laissez-faire*, liberal and socialist. These three possible welfare systems are ideal types. They have a descriptive usefulness in that they allow particular elements of social policy or welfare arrangements at a particular point of time to be identified as conforming to or diverging from each of the models. Then, in so far as they represent an internally consistent set of beliefs and actions, the models can also be used to explain both inconsistencies and contradictions within social policy and also trends in the development of legislation which can be related to the different systems.

I have used the three ideal types to analyse British arrangements and so demonstrate the patchiness of the welfare system, composed as it is of a historical accumulation of different responses to various powerful demands. There has emerged a collection of policies and practices approximating in some ways, and to a greater or lesser degree, to each of the models of *laissez-faire*, liberalism and socialism. Thus housing policy is based on market principles of distribution but modified by liberal and socialist elements, for example, in the provision of sheltered homes for the elderly or rent rebates for the poor. Education is a shifting compromise between the liberal principle of equality of opportunity, the *laissez-faire* principle of private enterprise and the socialist principle of positive discrimination. Health incorporates, similarly, both the citizenship right of universal access and the market principle of private medicine.

I have also used the same analytical approach to try to identify movements in various parts of the welfare system towards or away from one or other of the three models, paying particular attention to T. H. Marshall's thesis about the growing significance of the concept of citizenship. This kind of analytical procedure must be used with great caution, for it can easily be abused. First, there is the danger of accepting an extreme form of functionalist theory which could, however illicitly, be read into my discussion of welfare need especially where the unit to which the term 'need' is applied is a society or collectivity rather than an individual person. Second is the perhaps greater danger of succumbing to theories of mechanical history, two versions of which are in wide circulation among those who discuss issues of social policy and social administration.

With regard to functionalist theory, care is needed to avoid assuming too tight a correlation between elements of social structure which influence social distribution and the nature of social policy itself. Thus, for example, if a one-to-one correlation is assumed between the complexity of the division of labour and the provision of equality of educational opportunity, bureaucratically provided social-security benefits, or public-health care then there is no way of explaining variation in such services among societies with similar occupational structures. It is not that functionalism is a totally false theory, lacking in explanatory power, but rather that it can only be reconciled with the facts of social variation in its weaker forms. The explanation of variation has to be sought also in the peculiar historical, political and economic circumstances and character of a particular society at a particular time. Functionalist explanation cannot account for the way British social policy differs from any of the three implicitly functional models that I have used, and it must be supported by an analysis of the effects of belief and action in all relevant aspects of the social structure. Understanding of social policy, in other words, depends on judgements about the power of and relations between all those groups and organisations which influence distribution – governments, political parties, pressure groups, professional associations, and so on.

Nor should the use of the three models be misunderstood as suggesting that actual welfare arrangements are the more or less direct reflection of philosophical beliefs about the principles which should guide welfare distribution. Such an idealist or intellectualist theory has to be demonstrated and not assumed, and I do not want to advocate it. All that I intend to suggest by the three labels from this point of view is that belief and action may be usefully examined in terms of their mutual consistencies and inconsistencies, leaving it an open question as to whether, if they differ, action will alter to reflect belief or vice versa.

If we look at the situation in Britain now, for instance, it is immediately obvious that there is a large gap between many people's belief about the nature of the welfare state – what it does and what it ought to do – and the actual character of social policies. Most people would probably agree on the need to eliminate financial poverty, to bring about equal educational opportunities, to provide a healthy environment and adequate medical services for the population. Most people would also probably believe that by and large such objectives were being achieved, though the optimism of the 1950s has been challenged and partially undermined both by empirical enquiries which demonstrate the persistence of many forms of poverty and by the changing theoretical conception of poverty in terms of inequality and relative deprivation. I have tried to suggest in the last two chapters some of the measures that would be needed if the comfortable and moderately egalitarian beliefs about the efficacy of the welfare state were actually to be reflected in the extent and quality of public provision. We would need a more discerning definition of poverty and deprivation, more reliable ways of measuring it, a more certain conviction of what we want to do about it and a better understanding of how to achieve our objectives.

The second danger is an important one because of two politically opposed versions of a common historical fallacy which are frequently advanced. In the 1950s courses in social administration in British universities commonly subscribed to a belief, perhaps rather taken for granted, that the welfare state developed automatically as a result on the one hand of benevolence on the part of the politically powerful and on the other hand of the requirements of increasing industrialisation. An 'upwards and onwards' historical movement towards 'the end of ideology' was assumed, as was the erosion of class conflict and the increasingly sophisticated understanding and increasingly effective solution of 'social problems'. This unargued and untested theory provided an historical framework for cheerful descriptions of the development of the social services, with heavy emphasis on the increased resources allocated to them year by year, regret for the remaining deficiencies of provision, scant attention to the persisting inequalities in living standards, faith in the benevolent activities of larger and larger numbers of professionally trained social workers and confidence in ultimate progress towards a comprehensive welfare system. Any notion of conflict is notably lacking from this kind of interpretation. The possibility that some classes might oppose social redistribution or that the organised profession of social work might be in any way at odds with the receivers of welfare is seldom considered.

In contrast, and mainly outside the university departments of social administration and social work, Marxists offer an interpretation of the welfare state in terms of the more or less conscious endeavour of ruling classes to maintain their own power; to gentle the masses by repairing the more glaring injustices associated with capitalism. In this view not only are welfare measures ineffectual in bringing about any 'real' improvements, which must await a radical reordering of society, they are also mischievous in so far as they delay the development of full class-consciousness which must in any case occur and which will inevitably lead to revolutionary change. The dominant feature of this school of thought is that conflict is a necessary and sufficient cause of social change.

Both of these versions of historical determinism are still current, but neither experience nor the study of events makes them any the more plausible and both should be rejected. We need better explanations of the nature of social policy and better theories about the way in which changes may be brought about. It is essential to insist, in contrast to over-optimistic liberals and over-dogmatic Marxists, that the distribution of welfare and opportunities can be significantly changed by political action which stops short of revolution, but at the same time to recognise that the circumstances under which such changes can be effected are extremely complex. It is not only a matter of defining the aims and ideals of welfare policies, or of enacting benevolent legislation. Nor can it be assumed that improvements will automatically stem from the pressure and interests of the welfare profession. The power for change, as has emerged in the debate over the capacity of educational reform to realise goals of equality or even equality of opportunity, does not lie in the system of welfare alone but also in those other elements of the social structure, including family and community, to which I have referred in earlier chapters and which can themselves, of course, be influenced by political and administrative action. Intellectual ability and political skill are needed to define ends and devise practicable programmes for reaching them, and this demands an effective partnership between social research and political action. Finally, the more the power that passes to public bodies to order other men's lives, the more those organisations must become responsible to the people they are set up to serve and the more the care that must be exercised to safeguard the democratic rights of laymen from professional and bureaucratic authority. The development of social policy based on a conception of citizenship is a formidable challenge both to sociological imagination and to political resolve.

APPENDIX A

An Estimate of the Number of Persons in Poverty in 1970

At the end of 1970[1] the Supplementary Benefits Commission was making 2,738,000 weekly payments and thus supporting 4,166,000 persons.[2] The great majority, over two-thirds of those receiving benefits, were old people, 12 per cent were sick and disabled, 9 per cent were unemployed and a slightly smaller percentage were women with dependent children. Only 200,000 of the 2,738,000 receiving allowances had capital assets (apart from a house) of £500 or more. Altogether 897,000 persons had some other income and these were mainly retirement pensioners whose additional income was drawn mostly from capital assets or superannuation which provided on average £0.16 and £1.44 a week respectively.[3] In other words, very few of the four million persons regularly dependent on supplementary benefit were living far above the minimum standard it provides.

These are the persons known to be relatively poor. There are also, however, those who are drawing insurance benefits of one kind or another, who are not working and whose incomes are therefore likely to be below the assistance scales. At the end of 1970 only 28 per cent of retirement pensioners, 20 per cent of those having unemployment benefits, 15 per cent of those drawing sickness benefit and 16 per cent of those having widow's benefit also received supplementary benefit. However, it is the long-term claimants under the insurance scheme who are most likely to be poor. In 1970 there were 7,525,000 retirement pensioners and 595,000 drawing widow's benefits.

We have no firm information about the economic circumstances of widows – except of those who also draw supplementary benefit – but we have an official analysis of the situation of old people.[4] The figures relate to 1965 when there were 8 million men and women over pensionable age; 6,190,000 of these were retirement pensioners, and the remainder were mainly persons who were still working or the wives of men still working or receiving grants from the National Assistance Board. The majority lived on very low incomes; 48 per cent of married

174

couples had less than £10 a week and 54 per cent of single men and 67 per cent of single women less than £6 a week (National Assistance scales at that time allowed £3.80 a week and rent, for which the average payment was then £1.50, for a single householder). Besides those actually receiving assistance (18 per cent of married couples, 22 per cent of single men and 34 per cent of single women) substantial numbers of old people seemed eligible for but were not claiming it (11 per cent of married couples, 13 per cent of single men and 21 per cent of single women). In all, nearly two-thirds as many as were having assistance would have been entitled to it. There is no evidence that the situation has greatly changed.[5] Furthermore, according to the Ministry's survey there were 16 per cent of married couples, 27 per cent of single men and 20 per cent of single women who, although not qualifying for supplementary benefit, had incomes less than £1 above the scales. Altogether only 55 per cent of married couples, 38 per cent of single men and 25 per cent of single women of retirement age had incomes which were more than £1 above the minimum level.

If it can be assumed that in 1970 similar proportions of retirement pensioners were eligible for assistance but not claiming it, and similar proportions were living only just above the official minimum, this would mean that over and above the 2,296,000 supported by the Supplementary Benefits Commission there would be another three million or so old people below or only slightly above the poverty line.[6]

Many of the other supplementary-benefit allowances are likely to be short-term, but even if we discount altogether unemployment assistance we still find over one million persons supported by allowances to the sick and disabled and to widows and women with dependent children, leaving aside those who are eligible and who do not apply and those who are only just above the Commission's scales. So between 7 and 8 million people without earned income and living permanently around subsistence level in 1970 is probably an underestimate.

Apart from those receiving supplementary benefit, those eligible for it but not claiming it, and those who live only slightly above the standard, there is an important group who may have incomes insufficient for their needs judged by supplementary-benefit scales, but who may not be eligible for any benefits – the families of men in full-time work at low wages. Professor Atkinson, using Department of Employment and Productivity figures, shows that in 1968 3 per cent of adult men working full-time, that is nearly half a million men, had earnings which were less than would have been needed to support a wife and two children at the level then allowed by the Supplementary Benefits Commission.[7] 2 per cent, or 200,000 men, could not even support a wife and child at that level. These statistics do not, of course, give any measure of the number of persons living in poverty as a result of low earnings for there is no information about the size of the families of the men concerned. But they indicate that, even in a time of comparative prosperity, wages for some kinds of work were too low to support even a small family at the official minimum.

A more precise measure of the extent of poverty attributable at any rate in part to low wages is available for 1966 and contained in the report of a government-sponsored enquiry.[8] This survey was based on a sample of all families with two or more children who were receiving family allowances. It suggested that, of the total of 3.9 million such families in the country, 280,000 had initial resources (excluding any assistance allowances) which were below their needs as measured by assistance scales; 70,000 were the families of men in full-time work. Large families are much more vulnerable to poverty – 14 per cent of those with six or more children compared with 1 per cent of those with two children were below the supplementary-benefit scales. On the other hand, among the 70,000 in poverty (so defined) there were more two-child families than any other size and two- and three-child families together made up nearly half the total.[9] The 70,000 families contained 255,000 children. This suggests a total of around 400,000 persons living below assistance scales in 1966 and not eligible for assistance because the father was in full-time work; and it leaves out of account one-child families who might be in a similar position. The others below the assistance scale were 15,000 families who did not receive full rates because of the wage stop and another 75,000 who appeared eligible but did not receive anything – often the families of men who had been sick or unemployed for only a short period. In all, approximately 217,000 adults and 408,000 children were living below the assistance level and not receiving assistance.[10] These figures are an underestimate since they relate to only three million rather than the total of 3.9 million of families with at least two children. It seems likely that in all, nearly one million persons were living below the assistance scales – and this excludes the one-child families.

The overall total of persons living below or around the supplementary benefit level in 1970 would thus be between eight and nine million.

NOTES

1. The D.H.S.S. has published a report for 1972 (Cmnd. 53552) but the statistics are less comprehensive so earlier figures are quoted here. It should be noted, however, that the number of weekly payments had risen to 2,929,000 by November 1972.
2. *Department of Health and Social Security Annual Report 1970*. See p. 76.
3. Ibid. tables 125 and 126.

4. Ministry of Pensions and National Insurance, *Financial and Other Circumstances of Retirement Pensioners*.

5. Atkinson, *Poverty in Britain*, chap. 4.

6. This is a very uncertain guess failing more recent analysis of the age, sex, marital status and economic situation of pensioners.

7. Atkinson, *Poverty in Britain*, p. 80.

8. Ministry of Social Security, *Circumstances of Families* (H.M.S.O., 1967).

9. Ibid. tables 11.3 and 11.4.

10. Ibid. table A.1.

Index